A Welsh Uncle

This is Tom's story, because it falls short of a detailed biography, and as it's over sixty years since his death, few who knew him are alive.

The material and photographs have been assembled into a narrative from a number of Morgan family archives, together with various recorded memories, and supplemented with compilations from open sources and some newspaper cuttings.

The story idea developed after family research around 2008, and following a visit to Castello di Vincigliata in 2011 continued gathering momentum. In charting his progress it was necessary to occasionally speculate with small factual jig-saw pieces to form a mostly true story narrative. However any interpretations of events and characterisation surrounding the Morgan and extended families or his life, together with any mistakes are mine alone.

Like so many who play a part in life's production their involvement in certain events are often air-brushed out, receive no billing or acknowledgment.

For once Tom gets star billing, my tribute to a Welsh uncle.

A Welsh Uncle

First Published in 2018 by FastPrint Publishing Peterborough, England.

A CIP catalogue record for this book is available from the British Library

Paperback ISBN 978-178456-597-8

Printed and bound in England by www.printondemand-worldwide.com

www.fast-print.net/bookshop

Johndann25@gmail.com
Nansledan Cornwall

A Welsh Uncle

Memories of Tom Morgan
1898 – 1957

John Dann

Tom had the distinction of fighting in two world wars. In the first with the Royal Engineers and the second with the Royal Pioneer Corps taking part in many POW escape attempts

(Campo 12 -Italy)

"...while the remaining six officers (two VC's) and thirteen NCOs (including CQMS Thomas Morgan) and men went through hours of tedious watching to ensure (the tunnel's) success. Every one, officers and men, were in it, and wildly keen for success!"

Lt-Gen. Sir Philip Neame, V.C., K.B.E., C.B., D.S.O.,
extract from '*Playing with Strife, The Autobiography of a Soldier*'

(Stalag VIIA -Germany)

"The entrance to the tunnel was from under the last seat on the left in the latrine and it was strictly taboo to use it. One day a Greek Officer who ...absent-mindedly arranged himself on the forbidden seat only to be impaled in the arse on a home-made entrenching tool wielded by a furious Welsh tunneller (CQMS Tom Morgan) who caught him just in time."

Capt. D.W.D. Bond, M.C.,
extract from '*Steady, Old Man! Don't You Know There's a War On?*'

Contents

Prologue

On 29 February 1940 *Welsh Rarebit,* a thirty-minute radio variety programme, was first broadcast from Cardiff by the BBC. It featured a resident 25-strong male voice choir, the Lyrian Singers.

They performed a new song *We'll Keep a Welcome*, it was Tom's pre-war musical score sold to Idloes Owen, subsequently acquired by the programme's producer Mai Jones. She collaborated with Lyn Joshua and James Harper to create the lyrics. The song's rousing finale was an overnight success.

The show continued until 1952, featuring a host of Welsh entertainers, many of whom became household names such as; Eynon Evans, Gladys Morgan, Harry Secombe, and Stan Stennett. At its peak the programme attracted 12 million listeners, remaining one of the most popular entertainment shows produced from Wales. The show's most lasting legacy remains its closing song, *We'll Keep a Welcome*.

How Tom might have benefited from the success of his musical work had he retained copyright, we can only speculate. But his philosophy tells us,

"Life ain't all yer wants but, it's all yer 'aves,
Stick a geranium in yer 'at and be 'appy."

-1-

To begin at the Beginning

"I loved a man whose name was Tom, He was strong as a bear and two yards long"...

Polly Garter's song from Dylan Thomas's 'Under Milk Wood'

As a young boy growing up in Wales, Castles had a fascination and exploring them was an exciting pastime. The Principality has more castles per square mile than any other country in Western Europe, so there are many to visit.

They range from the majestic Caernarfon and Harlech in the North to Caerphilly, Chepstow and the 'fairy tale' Castell Coch in the South. They appear in many novels, mysterious, often as prisons, which inevitably included a rescue or an exciting escape. Many are just ruins now, like Pencoed castle, as the story goes our Morgan family ancestral home. They all come with stories and it is through this connection my interest in history was aroused. Tales of Welsh folklore hero like *Twm Sion Cati*, and during school holidays it would be a chance to explore historical sites on my 'trusty steed' -a Raleigh bicycle.

Pencoed, the 16th century 'Morgan' castle

Castell Coch, Radyr

It is perhaps not surprising as boys become men; they find there is something compelling and satisfying in restoring castles. The would-be (wealthy) owner can return them to their former glory whilst adding something of their own tastes to the building.

One of these was Castell Coch (which means red castle in Welsh); a few miles from Cardiff near the village of Tongwynlais, not far from the original Morgan family home in the Merthyr Valley. It was built in the neo-gothic style during the 1870s, on the site of an earlier thirteenth century Norman castle, for one of the wealthiest men in the land, John Crichton-Stuart, third Marquess of Bute.

On the Continent at much the same time, a wealthy Englishman Sir John Temple Leader had settled in Italy and embarked on restoring another castle, the thirteenth century Castello di Vincigliata a medieval ruin on a Tuscan hill at Fiesole eight kilometres north-east of Florence.

It was once the ancient stronghold of important Florentine nobility. Leader also re-built it in the neo-gothic style. After his death it passed through several owners until World War Two when it became a prisoner of war camp. It was naturally intriguing to discover that my favourite uncle had once been a prisoner there.

Castello di Vincigliata – as Campo PG 12, prisoner of war camp c.1946

Castello di Vincigliata – Fiesole, near Florence as an events venue and vineyard c.2011

The Morgan family

Thomas Henry Morgan, known as Tom, was born on Saturday 12 February 1898 at eight `o'clock in the morning under the sign of Aquarius; in his paternal grandparents' house at 40 Cardiff Road in the Welsh mining village of Merthyr Vale. It was where Margaret his older sister had been born three years earlier.

We know all this as grandmother would keep a meticulous record of all the births of her nine children. She was born Annie Wakely in 1874 in the village of Mountain Ash, the seventh child of Henry Wakely a miner and his wife Margaret. She had the Welsh mystical gift of *ail olwg* -second sight. Possibly through her mother she had also acquired knowledge of the beneficial use of mountain plants and became an affective herbalist. One of her remedies was a poultice or ointment that could clean, heal and erase those 'miners blue scars' –caused by fine coal dust infecting even minor scratches. In time she became involved with the local Nursing Association and with much person experience she often acted as a midwife to the village mothers.

She was teetotal and a member of the *Independent Order of Rechabites*, part of the wider British temperance movement, founded in early nineteenth century as a benefit society, whose members abstain from intoxicating liquors. However paradoxically she also enjoyed a glass of Stone's Ginger wine at Christmas! She frowned upon playing cards and would not have them in the house referring to them as "*cards of the devil.*" This didn't stop the Morgan sons' drinking or playing cards -out of sight of course!

Annie had met her future husband one summer day in Nelson a village near Treharris, at the lower end of the Taff Bargoed Valley. He was an amateur musician with the *Merthyr Vale & Aberfan Silver Band.* During a break in their performance they were given a lunch in the garden of the *Nelson Inn (now Lord Nelson)* on the Shingrig Road. She and her close friend Charlotte Harding –daughter of the Inn's owner were helping to serve the bandsmen. As young girls do, they dared each other to steal a silk handkerchief from the top pocket of one of the band members. Annie chose Tommy and Charlotte Harding another. Eventually they both married the victims of their prank.

Tom's grandparents – Josiah and Elizabeth

Tom's father, Thomas John Morgan was born in March 1873 in Walnut Tree Bridge Radyr village, five miles north of Cardiff; the youngest child of Josiah Morgan, a Puddler in an iron foundry, and Elizabeth Thomas, a dressmaker. Josiah was twenty and Elizabeth sixteen when they married in June 1870; she was illiterate, signing the registry with a 'cross'. She was also five months pregnant with her first son David born the same year. Lina his sister arrived the following year.

The family moved to Taff's Well and later to Canton in Cardiff. It seems home life was unhappy from the start for young Tom. His father away for prolonged absences and on his return was often violent to his mother. The violence had started almost at once when they first married and continued intermittently for the next fifteen years.

Josiah and Elizabeth Morgan c 1870s –an unhappy marriage

Elizabeth increasingly isolated and neglected, with little money looked for companionship with a certain David Thomas and another Harry Stacey in particular, which inevitably led to a divorce.

Eventually unable to cope with this family atmosphere, at the age of twelve Thomas ran away from home, and in January 1885 his mother was "*turned out of doors*" of the family house in 28 Pen-Y-Peel Road Canton. She was penniless and reduced to lodgings in various Cardiff brothels, Bute Terrace, Tudor Road and finally Habershon Street.

In December 1885 Josiah instigated divorce proceedings with a London solicitor Montagu Scott & Baker on the basis of her adultery.

A Cardiff Divorce Case, a Shocking Story [1]

In April 1887 the petitioner's case *Morgan v Morgan & Thomas* was heard in the High Court before Sir James Hannen, an old school Victorian judge, who expressed his view on marriage thus: "*…marriage represented protection on the part of man and submission on the part of the woman.*"

Cruelly perhaps the children were called as witnesses –the boys David (16) and Thomas (14) for their father, and Lina (15) for her mother. In her mother's defence Lina spoke of several physical assaults over a ten year period and told the court, that on many occasions he (Josiah) would tell her mother *"if she wanted food or money to go on the streets and earn it"* - coerced prostitution.

Elizabeth was represented by Cardiff solicitor George David. Despite her witness statement, and compelling evidence of persistent cruelty, the jury found the respondent and her co-respondent (David Thomas) guilty of adultery. They also found (unaccountably) the petitioner not guilty of cruelty or connivance. Hannen pronouncing a decree nisi in favour of Josiah and awarded damages of £75 (he'd asked for £250). It was remembered as a family cause célèbre and reported widely in the Cardiff and South Wales press.

Two years later, Josiah married Sarah Shepherd, twenty years his junior; the eldest daughter of Henry and Ann, farm labourers from the little village of Llandough. They settled at 2 Telford Street Canton where the first of her five children were born. Josiah was now a railway guard.

Elizabeth (using her maiden name) married Harry Stacey, a baker by trade and ten years younger, in the early spring of 1891. They lived at 70 Adam Street with her grown up children David, her married daughter Lina and husband John Garrett. Harry described them as his step-children. They moved to 1 Adeline Street, but sadly Elizabeth's new life was short lived, a few weeks after her daughter's second marriage, the earlier years of abuse and neglect caught up with her, at the age of forty-three she died of pelvic cancer and exhaustion in July 1897.

Tom's parents – Tommy and Annie

By the time his parents' divorce proceeding had completed, Thomas was living in Clive Place known as the 'Barracks' Merthyr Vale with his kindly aunt (Eleanor?) and uncle. They had no children of their own, and had arranged music lessons for him where he learned to play the cornet. He became a miner working at Nixon's Navigation Colliery (No.1 pit) in Aberfan.[2] Known as 'Tommy Cardiff' a typical Welsh nickname to differentiate the many similarly named; usually associated with their trade, mannerism or house location – in his case Mount Pleasant Cottage in the Cardiff Road.

Tommy had been captivated by Annie Wakely, (from the moment she took his handkerchief) and they married at Merthyr Tydfil registry office in February 1895. She was just three days short of her twenty-first birthday and seven months pregnant, with only her sister Harriet as witness (signing herself Morgan –not Wakely). Their first child Margaret was born the same year and Tom followed in 1898.

The family moved to Prospect House where their next three children, Arthur, Archie and George were born. Then in February 1905 they moved into a new six-roomed house at 8 Station Terrace, where the remaining Morgan children Maudie, Jess, Bernard and Lena Gwen were born. Tom's married sister Mag Rees's children Betty (1918) and Donald (1922) were also born there, a house full of love; it remained in the family for over seventy years. In contrast to his parents, Tommy and Annie had a happy marriage, *"a gentle man who never lifted a finger to anyone."*

Margaret (known as Mag) his older and closest sister had already left school and was working in the Merthyr Vale Post Office, for *"two fussy spinsters."* Later she took dress-making lessons in Aberfan. The teacher, Miss Sevenoaks, eventually asked her mother to take her away as she kept arguing with her; *"Just a minute Miss Sevenoaks, there's a better way to do that,"* or, *"if you put the pattern like this you'll save material."* [3]

So with these skills she was sent as a domestic servant to the Campbell's, a military family at Brimfield Hall, near Tenbury Wells.

John Campbell had a distinguished career, educated at Haileybury and Sandhurst. He was present at the *battle of Omdurman* in the Sudan, and awarded the Distinguished Service Order. He married Amy Leighton, third daughter of the Reverend Canon Hopkins.

Mag later moved to the Paton family in Penarth and by 1911 at the age of sixteen was serving in the Powell's household in Whitchurch.

One of her childhood friends Edith Hatton living at number fifteen a few doors down in Station Terrace had become a dressmaker.

In 1916 Edith invited Mag to her cousin Florrie's wedding in Blaengwynfi, a coal mining village near Neath in the Upper Afan Valley.

It was where Mag chanced upon another guest who was best friend of Jim Ware the bridegroom. He was Will Rees and they married a year later. Edith too found a husband and married Henry Small.

Annie and Tommy Morgan, c.1907

At the age of seven, young Tom had watched his father playing in the Merthyr Vale Silver Prize Band which won the Gwent Eisteddfod two years running in 1905-6. He played the cornet – the leading melodic instrument in this ensemble.

He was also remembered as a *cyfarwydd* -a storyteller in the old Welsh oral tradition. He would inevitably embellishing them with the re-telling; often, seeking confirmation from his wife-who would only assent with a non-committal murmur.

The Merthyr Vale Silver Prize Band with their conductor G H Thomas. Winners at the Gwent Eisteddfod in 1904 and 1905

Tommy Morgan, top row standing, second from left

Tom bottom row second from left, immediately above, sitting his father Tommy Morgan c.1911 (kind permission Jill Peck)

Tom the eldest son left Merthyr Vale School at the age of twelve, and followed his father 'down the pit' working at Nixon's Navigation described as a Coal Miner Boy (Filler).

Merthyr Vale was a new village that had grown up around the shaft development of John Nixon's colliery. It was completed in 1875, when the first commercial coal was brought up. The community expanded to create Aberfan, Nixonville and Mount Pleasant. Before that it was very much rural wales known as Ynys-Owen, the narrow valley was heavily wooded, either side of the river Taff, with various traditional Tyddyns long-house farms.

Tom and Mag were close village friends with two of the Owen family children. Richard and Jane, both fluent Welsh speakers lived in Crescent Street, later moving to Wesley Place. Their daughter Mary and son Idloes, were much their age –whilst his youngest brother born on 25 December was named Christmas!

Idloes had the voice of a boy soprano, like Tom he had joined his father down the pit as a collier. Tom and Mag continued their musical and personal friendship with him throughout their lives, and he went on to found the Welsh National Opera Company.

Left: 8 Station Terrace Merthyr Vale c.1910

Morgan children outside family home, 8 Station Terrace Merthyr Vale c.1907 (author)
Left to Right: Arthur (age 8), Tom (9), Maudie (baby in chair), Mag (12), Archie (5), George (2)

-2-
Picking primroses

"...Ask me why I send to you,
This primrose all bepearl'd with dew?
I will whisper to your ears: -
The sweets of love are mix'd with tears."

Robert Herrick, English poet

Yes I remember, because we picked a basketful of wild primroses that Saturday. Mum, Helene Dupont and I walked from Stumblehole upwards along the track to the Surrey woodland copse near Dene Farm, and for an hour or so we gathered enough primroses and moss to fill our garden trug for Uncle Tom's wreath.

Mum would take it with her on the train to his funeral the following Monday, he would be buried near Moreton in Marsh.

Mum was cook at Stumblehole the country house of Mayfair businesswoman Dorothy Hartman. Her artistic butler Frank Gear fashioned some chicken wire into a circle and patiently threaded the delicate primroses and moss together. When the wreath was complete, the yellow flowers, and green leaves on a bed of moss looked absolutely lovely. They were one of his favourite flowers.

Tom had died at five in the afternoon on Thursday 14 March 1957 in the home and presence of his daughter and son-in law at 2 Northwick Terrace, Blockley. He was fifty-nine. Mum his youngest sister, known as Lena Gwen, had been expecting the news for days. When the telephone rang she took the call (from Blockley 351) in the small partitioned glass panelled room next to the kitchen which housed the farm switchboard (Norwood Hill 123).

It was also the boot room and where the owners Pekinese dogs slept at night in their wicker baskets. As she listened to the call I sensed the inevitable, and joined her. She wept and we hugged each other at the sad news. It was my first recollection of a family death.

On returning home mum recalled a scene during the funeral that had upset the whole family. Winnie (known as Win by the Payne family) having nursed Tom in his final days, was understandably weeping - coincidently it was a day before her thirty-ninth birthday. Seeing her distress, Tom's estranged wife, the volatile Vi approached her and clearly out to make mischief, asked within hearing, "*Why are you making such a fuss?"* –heads turned, then she threw in a caustic remark "...*He wasn't your father anyway!"* [4]

Winnie was stunned by this sudden and unexpected revelation she had been completely unaware of this family truth. The resulting emotional scene was heard by all mourners, a spiteful and unnecessary cruel act. But Vi did have 'form'. Typical of the woman Mum and I had experienced before.

Mum was very fond of her eldest brother and to me without a living father or grandfather for reference; he was the sort of family hero that only appear in *Boy's Own* adventure stories.

A month earlier, Tom had an operation for stomach cancer at Cardiff Royal Infirmary. Afterwards he travelled to convalesce in the Cotswolds at the invitation of his daughter Winnie and her husband Ralph. It turned out to be a very short convalescence.

Just after his operation he had written a brief note from hospital, a day before his birthday which gives a glimpse of his personality and optimism.

Glan Ely Ward
Royal Infirmary
Cardiff

"Hello Gwen and Johnnie,

My first attempt at a letter since my operation. I'm out of bed for the first time -just for an hour. Gosh! I'm weak and my tummy feels as if it's tied in seventeen knots so, I'm not doing too much. I'm told I've got to get out and move around as much as possible to get the new system in my tum working. I expect Mag has kept you up to date with the bulletins.

But oh Gwen, I've had one hell of a time. And once fit and well and out of here I pray to God I may never have to come in again. It's stimulating and thrilling to see how the family has rallied round. Mag God Bless her has hardly missed a night. Muriel and George too and even Bern has been three times and Morfydd too. Leslie came yesterday and today.

Winnie is ringing every night. I arranged to go to Winnie's to convalesce when I get out. I'm afraid it will be a long time before I get back to normal. However I'm on the right road to recovery thank God. Thank you and bless you for those beautiful flowers. Everybody loved them. Don't worry any more Gwen Darling.
I must get back to bed now.

All my love to both you and John and God Bless.

Tom xxxx"

Thirty days later his death certificate would show he died of a combination of a congested heart disease and an inoperable carcinoma of the rectum.

Uncle Tom first entered my life when I was nearly two years old. He was forty-seven, having recently been repatriated from a prisoner of war camp in Germany. My grandmother had died suddenly just before Victory in Europe-VE Day in May. He arrived at the family house in Merthyr Vale later the same month – the first Morgan brother home from the war.

Grandfather had died in the months before the war, and from 1941, Mum had been living with her mother whilst working in the Royal Ordinance factory in Bridgend. Although her sister Maudie's children June and David stayed for a while, as did some billeted London Evacuees Marian and Pat. My mother married Jack Dann in September 1942; he was serving in the Royal Navy as a Petty officer. He was killed the following year when his ship was torpedoed in the Mediterranean a few months before I was born. After grandmother died it was not possible to maintain the old house as mum had little money.

About a year later we moved to Cardiff at Tom's invitation, to stay with him and his wife Violet – known as 'Vi', whilst mum looked for a housekeeping job. They had a small terraced house in the district called Adamsdown. It was a brief and unhappy time for us.

Vi had flame coloured auburn hair and a temper to match. They were divorcing and for some reason she became 'difficult' about my mother and I being there. This may have been the attention Tom gave us - his youngest widowed sister with a three year old son. Whatever the reason, Vi's temper was volatile. On one occasion it erupted -screaming at us whilst violently pulling my mother's hair. Naturally Tom intervened and the row calmed.

Inevitably in this uneasy atmosphere we would have to move on, which we did. Tom's marriage was over; no doubt the personal strains of separation and re-adjustment to post war life coupled with her temper took their toll. Mum used to say, *"Vi was insanely jealous."* We left Tom's and did not see him again for another five years.

Mum had found a temporary position for six months as housekeeper and nannie to the Hamilton's small child who lived in Newport Road, then later secured a permanent position as cook-housekeeper to a Doctor Joyce (said to be a distant relative of actress Joyce Grenfell). A general practitioner in his forties, living in 'WestWinds' a corner house in Penygroes Road, in the Cardiff suburb of Rhiwbina. We settled there for just over two years.

Then tired of his parsimony and unwanted attention we left for Badminton in rural Gloucestershire in the autumn of 1949, the same year the first Horse Trials were held. This time Mum had obtained a new appointment through the *Lady Magazine* as cook to Margaret, Lady Brassey, a granddaughter of the fifth Duke of Buccleuch and a distant relative of the Queen. Her husband, a Lieutenant-Colonel in the *First Life Guards*, had died a few years earlier. His Grandfather Thomas Brassey, a civil engineer, was responsible for building much of the world's railways in the nineteenth century. By 1847, he had built about one-third of the railways in Britain, and astonishingly by time of his death in 1870 he had built one mile in every twenty miles of railway in the world.

She lived alone, with Pekinese dogs in the Old Vicarage at the western end of the village High Street, part of the 10th Duke of Beaufort's estate. Mother and I didn't live in the main house – but were given a small two room hut in the kitchen garden which we shared with Queen Mary's cat. During the war, the old Queen had temporarily moved from London to Badminton House, staying with the Duke and Duchess for her safety. After the war she returned to Clarence House but her cat stayed. It was a large and eccentric tabby who adopted my mother. He would only enter through a window leaving paw marks on the wallpaper underneath, sleeping at the bottom of her bed. By some unknown telepathy the cat would wait for us and escort us (at a distance) home from the local bus stop, sometimes late at night as we caught his eyes in our torch light, after our occasional (monthly) day-out to Bristol or Bath (Mum preferred the shops in Bristol).

We settled into Badminton village life and mum was enticed into the Women's Institute. I attended the local school and became a chorister at the eighteenth century church of *St Michael and All Angels*. After a while mum became increasingly worried about my education – or the lack of progress I seemed to be making in the little village school.

The Old Vicarage Badminton

So at the age of seven, I was sent to live with my Aunt Mag in Cardiff where the education was considered much better. My mother hoped that in this atmosphere of learning and education –some of it would rub off on me. I was to stay for three years.

Mag lived in Dogfield Street in Cathays. She had four grown up children, the eldest daughter Betty had read modern languages at University in late 1930s (*College Hall Llanishen* then *Aberdare Hall*) and Margaret the youngest (always known as Micky) a brilliant young scholar, at Cathays High School, had matriculated to Cardiff University after the war where she read modern languages –played hockey, was captain of the women's athletics team, graduating with a Bachelor of Arts degree.

The eldest son, Donald (Don) had served as a wireless operator in the RAF, in *504 Squadron* in Rhodesia during the war. Young Russell who was just seventeen, had joined the 7th Battalion *Royal Welsh Fusiliers*, getting wounded fighting his way through the Reichswald Forest just before the final advance on Germany. Later he served with the British Army of Occupation (B.O.A.R) with the *South Wales Borderers.* [5]

Both now demobilised, they had married and pursued different careers. Don became a teacher and moved to Leeds where he also played rugby league for *Hunslet.* Both Betty and Margaret were also teachers, only Russ joined the commercial world with Rank Hovis McDougall.

Her husband Will Rees had been a miner with the *Ocean Coal Co.* in West Glamorgan. The family then lived at 29 Villiers Road Blaengwynfi, before moving to Cardiff briefly during the General Strike in 1926 staying for a while in Diamond Street Splott. They returned permanently in 1940 to Dogfield Street in Cathays.

Will was now working as a civil servant at the Ministry of Transport in Newport Road. Previously he had worked on the university building during the 1920s when the coal industry was in recession. He'd often point to the green dome on the building roof whilst out walking – saying *"look up there boy, I helped build that."*

When I was eight, he took me to watch the young Cliff Morgan, in his 1951 debut international against Ireland playing at the Cardiff Arms Park. Tickets were like 'gold dust' for Internationals and I remember the 'sleight of hand' at the narrow spectators' entrance booth. Billo quickly slapped down a cover torn from a Players cigarette packet with something like a couple of half-crowns coins on top. With a conspiratorial nod to the attendant –who I believe was a friend from the British Legion, and click of the turnstile we walked into the stadium.

Cliff Morgan went on to be the star of the Lions Tour of South Africa in 1955, described as the best fly-half ever to visit, he became a Welsh legend.

This is the time I met Uncle Tom again. Now in his fifties separated from his wife (the vitriolic Vi) and lodging in the ground floor middle room of Aunt Mag's Cardiff house.

The Castle wall alongside Duke Street with St John the Baptist Church foreground

The legendary Arms Park rugby ground, where I saw Cliff Morgan play, with the Glamorgan cricket ground behind the stand

-3-

The house on the corner

...was host to Cardiff's war-time artistic and musical community

Aunt Mag the eldest of Tommy and Annie Morgan's children was very artistic, inheriting her grandmother's skills as a dressmaker. She enjoyed music and the company of cultured people, she knew Clara Davies, mother of composer Ivor Novello, and loved beautiful things – unfortunately without the funds for the latter.

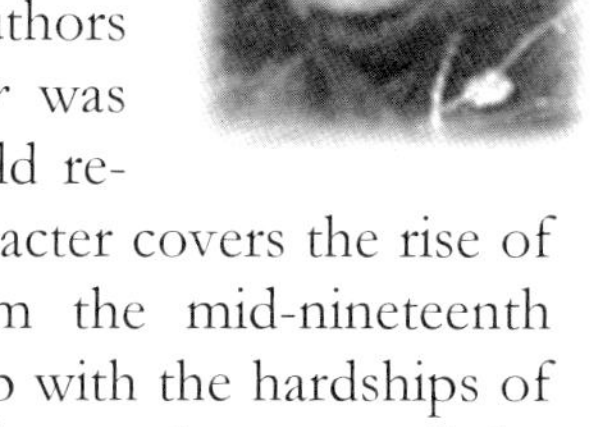

I can recall one of her favourite authors Howard Spring, whose novel *Fame is the Spur* was published at the beginning of the war. She would re-read each year. The book through its central character covers the rise of the socialist labour movement in Britain from the mid-nineteenth century to the 1930s. Part of the book is taken up with the hardships of life for coal mining communities in South Wales at the turn of the twentieth-century –something she could clearly identify with.

Among the popular film actors of the time, she was fond of Claude Rains who appeared in the romantic drama 'Casablanca' in 1942.

Cardiff in the 1950s like many other ports was recovering from war, and starting to be rebuilt. The city had boomed in the nineteenth century on the export of coal and iron. At its peak, the port had one of the largest dock systems in the world. Where the fast flowing river Taff black with coal dust washed down from the coal mines further up the valleys, made its way to the sea past the fabled Arms Park ground.

The castle dominated the centre –rebuilt by the Marquis of Bute –whose political and business influences were everywhere. It was a city that flowed with cultures from many nations, mixing with the local Anglo-Welsh society. The post-war gloom was lifted temporarily by the night neon displays from the cinemas of Queen's Street, and the shop picture window displays of Howell's and David Morgan [6] departmental stores along St Mary's street. Wales was struggling to establish its identity from an overshadowing neighbour, and it wasn't until 1955 that Cardiff was made the capital of Wales.

During the War years of the 1940s her corner house at twenty-five Dogfield Street became a meeting place for some of Cardiff's intellectual and musical society. She had a wide circle of friends including Idloes Owen the founder of the Welsh National Opera, a childhood friend from the same village, Merthyr Vale. He'd been Mag's one time boy-friend. She had even been engaged to him before meeting and marrying Will Rees in 1917, a gunner in the *Royal Field Artillery* during the Great War.

Idloes *(see image)* was very musical, originally a collier who had been diagnosed with tuberculosis. He left the mines and village neighbours raised money to send him to Music College to develop his talent. He became a composer, arranger and conductor; and considered possibly the finest singing teacher in Wales. Geraint Evans (1922-1992) the Welsh bass-baritone was one of his pupils.

Her younger brother Tom had a fine tenor voice and was a member of the Cardiff Dramatic and Operatic group called the *Lyrian Singers.* In 1943 it became *The Lyrian Grand Opera Company*, quickly changing its name to the *Welsh National Opera Company.* All created by Idloes Owen and a small group of enthusiasts.

Tom acted and sang in their various pre-war productions of operettas and little musicals, collaborating with composing various songs. One of the tunes Tom had composed – is the now universally known welsh standard *We'll keep a welcome.*

As the family story goes, Tom needed money so Idloes arranged to buy the copyright for a few pounds. Eventually the score passed to Mai Jones who is credited with the music, and Lyn Joshua and James Harper who later added the Lyrics.

During the late thirties, there had been a growing expectation of war. By the late summer of 1939, Neville Chamberlain, the British Prime Minster made a broadcast on the BBC Home service (now Radio 4). It was Sunday morning 3 September, and the nation held its breath, listening to his announcement at 11.15am:

"I am speaking to you from the Cabinet Room at 10 Downing Street. This morning the British Ambassador in Berlin handed the German Government a final note stating that, unless we hear from them by 11 o'clock that they were prepared at once to withdraw their troops from Poland, a state of war would exist between us. …"

He ended his broadcast with, *"Now may God bless you all. May He defend the right. For it is evil things that we shall be fighting against - brute force, bad faith, injustice, oppression and persecution - and against them I am certain that right will prevail."* Tom was forty-one, considered too old to join up, but by putting his age down had volunteered for the Army. By the time his music was establishing itself with listeners; he was on a troop ship bound for North Africa.

Amongst Cardiff's intellectuals and musicians at the time, were people like Mai Jones, a Welsh songwriter, entertainer and producer. She had won a scholarship to study music at the University of Wales. In

1941, she joined the BBC in Cardiff as a radio producer of light entertainment programmes such as *Welsh Rarebit* a radio variety show first broadcast in 1940. She wrote other songs – but none that has caught the public imagination like (Tom's) *We'll keep a welcome.*

Another was Wynford Vaughan-Thomas, (a favourite with Aunt Mag) a Welsh radio broadcaster. Born in Swansea he had been taught English at his school by Dylan Thomas's father. There was also a group of intellectuals and artists, the so called Kardomah [7] set who met at the café in Castle Street. It hosted the likes of Dylan Thomas (who spoke no Welsh) –the language used for his poetry was Anglo-Welsh, another poet Vernon Watkins, a bank clerk, the painter Alfred Janes a school-friend of Thomas (painted his portrait in 1934) and Daniel Jones an up and coming composer. During the war Wynford established his name and reputation as one of the BBC's most distinguished war correspondents. He later became one of the founders of Harlech TV now ITV Wales. He wrote numerous books on Wales and his love of the Welsh countryside. Amongst this group, Mag kept in touch with Idloes's sister Mary who lived nearby in Roath Park and they would often take tea together.

When I arrived at her six room Victorian house in the summer of 1951 it was full of people. Typically of many terraced houses in the district with bow sash-windows, located on the corner with Robert Street. It had a low wall separating the front of the house from the pavement that once used to feature wrought iron railings – long since cut down to help the previous war effort. The coloured mosaic floor tiles led to the porch, where the front door letterbox, was large enough to insert a hand enabling a string release to the catch. The hallway and staircase, a front room contained an upright piano, and stool full of sheet music, a middle room with fan-light and half-glass door to the garden, and back kitchen. There was a small yard with a large Rowan tree (Mountain Ash) in the corner that I used to climb, enjoying sitting amongst the branches. At the rear, another corner a house in Malefant Street backed on to the garden and occupied by the Erikson family. The father was the Norwegian consul in the city and I used to play with his daughter Christine. In the same street lived Gladys and her husband Percy – the middle daughter of Great-Grandfather Josiah Morgan's second marriage to Sarah Shepherd. [8]

Dogfield Street ran down to the local shopping parade in Crwys Road, where you would find the *Maypole Dairy*, grocers *Home & Colonial*, drapers *Bon Marche* and *Court's furnishings.* The road still had old tram lines, now used by trolley-buses on their route from Gabalfa to the city centre, and on to Pier Head in Butetown; the infamous Tiger Bay docklands, now redeveloped and known as Cardiff Bay. I was to share the back bedroom her husband Will – since a small child I'd always called him 'Billo'. The room had two single beds, a little fireplace, with its chimney wall festooned with war memorabilia, daggers, swords and trophies brought back from Germany by Russ after the war.

Aunt Mag had her 'boudoir' in the middle bedroom. To me she was a surrogate Grandmother and I loved her dearly. She was an ample and tactile woman, a comfort to a young boy needing a 'bit of cwtch' (hug). She often kept her long grey-white hair swept up and back held in a bun. For some inexplicable reason this used to remind me of Nurse Edith Cavell.

Her husband Will was a quiet man with a droll sense of humour but largely introvert when sober. Tolerant too, having just watched him fill the coal scuttle as a small child, I once threw the contents back at him from the top of the cellar steps. Another time near bonfire night, asleep in a chair, with aunt and mother deep in conversation, I had stuffed his sleeves and trousers with newspaper preparing him 'as a guy' –but was stopped using the matches.

A story often recalled about him at family gatherings was a war-episode during the Cardiff blitz. As the siren announced an air-raid he shouted up the stairs of an elderly woman neighbour urging her to hurry to the shelter, only to be told that she couldn't find her teeth.

Despite repeated calls she still responded about searching for her teeth. In exasperation, Will finally shouted, *"they (the Germans) were dropping bombs not bloody sandwiches!"*

Image: Author with Billo at a Civil Service summer event

At home he usually relaxed by taking off his collar and tie; revealing his white collar-less shirt, underneath his work black waistcoat with pockets containing *Rennie* indigestion tablets in white paper twists. He had greying swept back hair and a slightly yellowing moustache (a life-time of smoking *Woodbines*). On his watch-chain he kept a little promotional item –a miniature *Watney's* red beer barrel. On meeting, he usually opened with a question – "*olright then boy?"* and an exclamation "*by damn"* when something seemed beyond his comprehension. In winter he would take me to occasional matches at the Arm's Park the fabled Rugby ground. In summer we'd sometimes watch Glamorgan play cricket, where the famous opening batsmen of the day Gilbert Parkhouse and Bernard Hedges would entertain the crowds.

The house conversation was a mixture of Anglo-Welsh as was typical then. My Grandparents and great grandparents were all bi-lingual. However Cardiff, as major Welsh port was more cosmopolitan, Welsh had been assimilated into everyday conversational English and readily understood. Words such as; *Cariad* (love), *Bach* (little), *cwtch* (hug, cuddle), *Gwely* (bed), *Mochyn* (pig), *Hiraeth* (longing) and *Nos Da* (good-night); occasionally told to put a bit of *Hwyl* into it boy-*bach*, and not unusual to hear my name linked to the expression '*duw annwyl*' (dear God), probably by something I did? Because of its geography Wales receives a lot of rain, and many expressions to describe it, such as *Bwrw glaw* (raining pouring) –perhaps unsurprisingly also the name of a popular Welsh Nursery Rhyme.

The house had no telephone but as was usual in those days, the corner shop opposite would take messages (Cardiff 20283). Although referred to as Lewis's, it had been taken over by the Wilkins family, Selwyn and his wife Eileen, whose son Robert, went on to become a doctor and a life-long friend.

During term time there were three university students, all Welsh-speaking girls (Micky was in a hall of residence at this time) lodging with Aunt Mag, they shared the front bedroom. Their names were Nan, Mai-lynne and Ceinwen. The extravert out of the three was the blonde haired Mai-lynne. I remember that they found their lodging address and location hilarious – DOG-field Street in CAT-hays! They were as much attracted to Tom's charm as I was.

One evening I escorted Aunt Mag by trolley bus to the newly opened Sophia Gardens Pavilion where a performance of Puccini's *Madama Butterfly* was being staged. Once safely in the foyer, I turned to return home. She called me back and unexpectedly asked if I would like to see the performance with her. I readily accepted.

Then whilst mingling with the other opera lovers, she fell in to conversation with a group she knew. After a while one of her acquaintances turned to me and asked if I knew who wrote *Madama Butterfly*. *"Yes"* I said confidently. *"Shakespeare!"*

Tom had a rugged lived-in face, a rounded 'Morgan' nose, a warm smile, dimples either side of his mouth and a lovely speaking voice. He always called me Johnnie, it was different and I liked it.

He was different too - personifying a certain urbane charm – wearing dark coloured shirts in the artistic and bohemian way –not the conventional white. He was just slightly down-at-heal at this stage in a life that was once it seemed filled with adventure.

He'd been a soldier who had fought in two world wars, and had been a prisoner in a castle! Coupled with his involvement in the chorus of the up and coming Welsh National Opera Company, -all added to his romantic image.

The opera company started during the war, by a small group of enthusiastic music lovers led by Mag's friend Idloes Owen, who lived in Llandaff. Their first season of full opera was held after the war in April 1946 at the *Prince of Wales Theatre*, Cardiff when as Musical Director he conducted its first performance - *Cavalleria Rusticana.* (The Welsh tenor Robert Tear started his career as a schoolboy in this performance).

Later the WNO established another centre in Swansea and by 1951 the company had made its first tour of Wales. Such was the popular success of the first productions, applications poured in from people hoping to join the Chorus. They were all amateurs, coming from different walks of life, but all sharing a love of singing. It was said from the outset that the Chorus produced a very special quality of sound, unequalled by any other opera company. This quality was consistent - despite the fact that there were now two choruses, one serving Cardiff the other Swansea.

It was to this exciting Welsh musical venture that after his war-time captivity, Tom gave himself wholeheartedly. His love of music –a Welsh inheritance encouraged by his father, himself a successful amateur musician. By all accounts he seemed to live for singing and music. At this time he was working as a storekeeper and dispatch clerk in *James Howell & Co* a large department store in St Mary's Street, which was still a family firm in the 1950s.(Now part of House of Fraser)

I struck up a natural friendship with Uncle Tom, (he was really old enough to be my grandfather) he was easy to talk to and both of us; separated from our own families in different ways found enjoyment in each other's company.

1953 Churchman's advertisement

'The negotiable cards…

…and the smell of the greasepaint'

He used to smoke *Churchman's No 1* cigarettes. These cigarettes may have had a certain appeal to Tom. As magazine advertisements of the time would often feature a sophisticated woman on the telephone turning her head and saying; "*Darling – do give me a Churchman's No 1*" - all very theatrical, with perhaps a whiff of double entendre!

I would collect the cards that came with every packet (These were very negotiable at my school in Roath Park). By comparison they must have been a glorious smoke compared to the ersatz cigarettes he was often reduced to in various prisoner of war camps.

Prisoners would receive Red Cross parcels from time to time containing tea, other tined food stuffs and usually some cigarettes. He would continue to re-use the tea-leaves until the water became colourless – then, he would dry the leaves roll them in paper and smoke them.

He taught me how to pick a mortise lock with a piece of wire and by using a special rope knot to escape from a high window. The design of the knot would allow the escaper to release the rope from the ground, leaving no tell-tale signs. All learnt from his time as a prisoner in the castle. Sadly I've forgotten both skills!

Sometimes sitting together in his room talking, with the door open to the back yard, he'd pause and murmur, *"Listen Johnnie"*- quietly we'd hear the sound of a blackbird singing in the rowan tree. He told me in Italy the last days in January, are known as *"Giorni della merla"* –'the days of the blackbird', predicting forthcoming spring weather, for some reason their bird-song reminded him of freedom, *"free as a bird"* he'd say.

New Theatre Park Place Cardiff late 1950s

Tom outside 32 Dogfield Street 1955 (author)

For the opera productions he used stage make-up, and I would marvel at these *Leichner* [9] grease sticks kept in a drawer of a little dressing table in his room. They came in a flat brown cardboard box, together with the circular tins of stage blending powder. It was my first smell of greasepaint, which I found intoxicating, a smell I've never forgotten.

His theatrical white stage collars would sometimes be stained by brown greasepaint – and I would often be sent to deliver and collect them from a Chinese laundry in Gabalfa.

For one of my birthdays at Dogfield Street I was given a cowboy outfit by Aunt Mag made from bits and pieces of spare material; put together on her Singer treadle sewing machine. It had a brown felt hat, leather waistcoat, neckerchief and trouser-chaps complete with a toy 'six-shooter' and holster. I remember one day the revolver had disappeared only to re-appear again much later, as Tom had borrowed it to use as a stag prop for one of the parts in *Carmen?*

Looking back I believe that Uncle Tom's presence in that crowded house was beginning to be a strain for Mag. He was probably the cause of some friction and possibly a little jealousy between Mag and her husband Will Rees. Tom and Will were different personalities – Will liked watching rugby (his son Don played hooker and had a trial for Wales), a drink (or two) with his friends at the British Legion and on Saturday (with the room hushed) listening to the football results on the wireless, whilst checking his Littlewood's pools coupon.

Tom on the other hand was different. In company, his rich tone and speech would often include the theatrical endearment *"Darling"*; he was naturally charming and artistic, still enjoying Mag's sibling protection. However, his bohemian life-style and theatrical involvement in which she revelled, was being 'talked about' as an unsuitable environment for the 'sheltered' Welsh students Mag had lodging with her. More to the point one of them had developed a crush on him!

To John from Uncle Tom

Life ain't all yer wants but; it's all yer 'aves
Stick a geranium in yer 'at an' be 'appy.

Uncle Tom
– Jan 1st 1953.

For Christmas 1952 Aunt Mag gave me an autograph book. Naturally over the holidays I asked everyone I knew to write something in its blank pages. Tom scribbled his life's philosophy.

I recall conversations with mum that Tom didn't care much for a fellow Welsh singer, the up and coming baritone Ivor Emmanuel. A much younger man who would later be remembered for his part as 'Private Owen' in the 1964 epic film *Zulu* - the stoic defence at Rorke's Drift in 1879 during the Anglo-Zulu War.

At the age of twenty he had been helped by influential friend Richard Burton to secure a part in the original London production of *Oklahoma*, in the late 1940s staged at the *Theatre Royal, Drury Lane.* It launched his career. By the early 1950s he was singing in the *D'Oyly Carte* chorus, and Tom thought "*he was too full of himself*", and a "*womaniser*". This may have been because his marriage to a fellow-chorister was in difficulty which ended in divorce. Enough reasons perhaps to feed any feelings of jealousy. Perhaps, it was his ambivalent feelings towards Emanuel's link with the so-called 'Swansea Tafia' -a clique of artists and actors like Dylan Thomas, Richard Burton and Stanley Baker who had emanated from the area.

All may have been a little disingenuous perhaps, because I remember mum and me receiving a postcard from the sea-side town of Tenby in Carmarthenshire. Appropriately the birthplace of larger than life Welsh Bohemian artist Augustus John; where Tom was taking a short holiday with a 'lady friend' – John would have approved!

1953 was the year of the Queens' coronation – I remember little of it, mum was still busy in London, but recall sweet rationing had ended earlier the same year. My coupons had long been effectively requisitioned since arriving in Dogfield Street. I remember the freedom of spending a lot of pocket money (about a shilling) buying sweets from Wilkins corner shop and storing them in a jam-jar.

During the three years stay with Aunt Mag, mum had moved from Badminton, the isolation and boredom of country life didn't suit her and she felt very lonely. This time she had a position in the heart of London's Belgravia as cook to Sir Edward and Lady Ford, in Chester Square, one of London's premier addresses.

He was private secretary to Princess Elizabeth, later the Queen. His American wife Virginia born to Phyllis one of the five Langhorne sisters, was a niece of Lady Astor. The months building up to the coronation was a busy time for mum in the Ford household with a heavy schedule preparing and delivering many private dinner parties and the catering needs for their social entertaining.

Mum related an amusing –but embarrassing occasion when she was presented with other servants to Princess Elizabeth. She had been invited to a private dinner party in Ford's nineteenth century fashionable town house. The entrance hall was relatively narrow, and on being introduced she curtsied, accidentally cannoned off the wall behind nearly knocking the Princess over. Amongst her papers are some typed recipes one in particular exotically headed: *"Crayfish in a Brandy Mornay Sauce – for Twenty"*, Method: *"take ten boxes of frozen Danish crayfish..."*

During the winter of 1953-4 I had sat the eleven-plus school examination, learning in the summer that I had won a place at *Fitzalan Technical High School* - thus vindicating mum's decision to send me to Cardiff for the education.

By now I was really missing her; the years with Ford's London household had been demanding, and completely exhausted by personal events, she decided to move back to Cardiff. The students had left, Aunt Mag now in her late fifties was finding things difficult and getting frequently tired (she'd had a mild stroke). So her eldest son Don came to share the house. Bringing his wife Marion and four-year-old son Stephen, they established themselves on the ground floor.

In the summer Mum and I took lodgings - two rooms across the road at number thirty-two with Mrs Baker a kindly lady, and her daughter Doris. Tom had moved as well, taking lodgings in a small upstairs back bedroom in a house further along Dogfield Street at number hundred and five.

Mum had had found a catering job in the *Still Room* at David Morgan's *Oak Room Restaurant*, a family run department store in the Hayes. Money was tight and we had little to live on. This was made more difficult on one occasion as I had accidentally pushed about five shillings in loose change through a gap inside the base of a wall cupboard into the plasterwork underneath. Despite every effort we could not extract the coins. Tom came to our rescue by 'tunnelling' through the plasterwork and retrieving the money. He expertly covered the hole with a spare piece of wallpaper made good with a flour and water paste.

Around this time mum had managed to obtain (on Hire Purchase) a new Philips wireless. I used to study the dial stations like *Hilversum*, *Athlone* and *Luxembourg,* trying to locate them on my school atlas. Unfortunately its built-in aerial gave a poor reception. Tom with his practical resourcefulness made us a much more effective one. The aerial wire reached to the ceiling of our living room slipped through the garden door fanlight and then strung up high to a pole at the end of the back yard some ten yards away.

Shortage of money again loomed with the prospect of having to buy a school uniform. Tom offered to help by supplying my school cap. Unfortunately he bought the wrong one. Only knowing the school was in Howard Gardens, the shop assistant had presented the *Howardian High* cap with its pink strips. An easy mistake as the newly established *Fitzalan High* had only twelve months earlier taken over their old school building.

Its post-war repairs made good and the top floor sealed off after incendiary-bomb damage during the Cardiff blitz in 1941. *Howardian High* originally established to feed the newly opened university in 1885, had moved to its new site in Colchester Avenue Penylan.

This was all too confusing for Tom. By the time my mother could make it to the school's outfitters *Messrs. Roberts* in the Kingsway, they had sold out. My first day at school in September was cap-less and this embarrassment was compounded by the derision of my new peers!

However, I found Tom's empty Churchman cigarette tins very useful at school. I would collect the remains of discarded cigarette butts and carefully extract the un-smoked tobacco. All brands mixed together then machine rolled using Rizla papers marketed as the 'Fitz brand'. I would then sell to older boys, earning the sobriquet 'Dog-End' Dann. My tobacco venture came to an abrupt end on being discovered, earning 'six-of-the-best' as the thrashing was called.

In July the same year the founder of the WNO, Idloes Owen had died in the Royal Infirmary, leaving his wife Beatrice a widow. "*Idloes was loved by everyone and mourned by us all when he died. He was quiet, understated, and absolutely brilliant. He never lost his temper and his brain never stopped working on how to get a successful production to the stage. He was completely dedicated to music: it was everything to him.*" [10]

The company had now made its new temporary home at the *New Theatre* in Cardiff. Tom sang in the chorus for their first two week season at the beginning of November; which saw the production of eight opera's including two performances of *Nabucco.*

One evening the following year, Tom met the actor Derek Bond by chance in St Mary's Street. They had last seen each other ten years earlier in a German prisoner of war camp. Needless to say it became a grand impromptu reunion full of reminisces and many drinks.

Derek Bond *(see post-war publicity photo)* twenty years Tom's junior had been a repertory actor, but when war was declared joined up and was selected for officer training in the *Grenadier Guards.*

He served in North Africa, was wounded winning the Military Cross. Later he was captured in Florence in the summer of 1944 and sent to Stalag VIIA in Germany where he met CQMS Morgan.

Tom had already made as many as eight escape attempts and become the target for German reprisals. He'd been badly beaten by the Wehrmacht Guards and one Sicherheitsdienst (SS) officer in particular. Years later he told my mother if he ever met that man again – he'd kill him! Mum believed the punishment beatings he received in the camp brought on his stomach cancer – although probably the lack of proper nutritional meals and heavy smoking were contributory. Both prisoners were repatriated at the end of the war and went their separate ways.

Derek Bond resumed his career in film and theatre. He stared in film roles such as: *Nicolas Nickleby* (playing the leading role) in 1946, *Scott of the Antarctic* 1948 (he played Captain Oates), *Trouble in Store* in 1953 – Norman Wisdom's first film and many others.

In 1955 he had arrived in Cardiff, with a touring production of a stage play he'd written a year before called *Akin to Death*. It was staged at the *Prince of Wales theatre*, a theatre long since closed and now a Wetherspoon's pub of the same name. After this reunion Tom managed eventually to make it up the street as far as our lodgings late the same night - 'three sheets to the wind' and much the worst for wear. Mum looked after him and nursed his hangover. We eventually heard some fragments of the evening reminiscing and the camp story about the dog. As a result, Mum received some complimentary theatre tickets for one the evening performances. I was allowed to accompany her -it was my first theatre play and must admit to teenage boredom.

After this episode she would invite him to join us for Sunday lunch each week to make sure he had a decent cooked meal – at least once a week as he was neglecting himself, smoking more than eating.

I remember we both loved blackcurrant tart, one of his favourite puddings. I would be sent up the street on a Sunday morning after church (Altar boy at *St. Michaels & All Angels*) to his lodgings to remind him.

His landlady would open the front door and I would climb the stairs to his back bedroom. Knocking on the door quietly, opening it slowly calling out his name. The smell of stale tobacco was always present as was a full ash-tray on his bedside table. Sometimes he would be awake and say *"Hello Johnnie"* as I entered, at other times he would just grunt acknowledgement from under the bedclothes. Around this time Tom had become depressed – probably amongst other things the cancer was beginning to establish itself.

In the late autumn, Mum and I gave him a paperback re-print of Carton de Wiart's memoirs *Happy Odyssey*, bought initially as his Christmas present. She thought the 'read' would cheer him up because she knew the officer had been in the Italian prison camp with him. However, it did the opposite. He didn't really like the book, nor had much time for the officer.

We didn't understand his reasons then. Since reading the book I can sense from Carton de Wiart's personality that perhaps he did not have the same kind of empathy with other ranks as his fellow officers.

By now his health must have been deteriorating; but despite this I remember he always presented himself in a smart and tidy manner instinctively shoulders back 'military style' as he walked down the street raincoat over his arm, towards the Crwys Road bus stop.

The Welsh National Opera was going from strength to strength, which cumulated in their first London season in the summer of 1955 at *Sadler's Wells theatre* in Islington. One of the oldest theatres in London it had been a music hall fifty years earlier, where the bohemian Welsh artist Augustus John –then a student at the Slade, would regularly fling his hat in the air whenever he approved of a turn. [11]

Tom sang in the amateur chorus again at *Sadler's Wells* in July 1956 performing two Verdi opera's *Nabucco* and *I Lombardi* and Wagner's *Lohengrin.* They enjoyed rave reviews. The *South Wales Argus* editor Kenneth Loveland (Stroller) was present and wrote under the headings, *"Tradition Puts On A New Costume…Stroller's Saturday Night At The Opera"* reporting they had been an outstanding artistic success, producing record box-office figures.

> *"To-night, among working-class streets of the Angel, Islington, I was privileged to witness a body of men and women doing more for Wales than all your sounding harps…..or tub-thumping politicians."*
>
> *"……..Verdi's forgotten opera 'I Lombardi' had just reached its sonorous climax with spine-chilling sound – and London stood up to cheer. I forgot how many curtains the company took: was it eight or nine….? Did the very U-looking holders of orchestra stall tickets always behave in this outrageously enthusiastic fashion?"*
>
> *"How do they do it?" asked an opera lover who had visited all the great Continental opera houses. "How do they get such Pep, precision and complete and utter abandonment into their singing? Your chorus seems (if that's possible) to enjoy it more than we!"* [12]

All this from enthusiastic amateurs who came from all over South Wales to rehearse twice a week in a Cardiff garage in Frederick Street; and for this week, were just given a free rail ticket to London with eight guineas expenses! Sadly this season was to be Tom's last.
It was not until many years later, the Chorus became fully professional and today it is regarded as one of the finest in the world.

At the same time, my mother tired of low pay and the struggle of trying to make ends meet had applied for jobs as a cook housekeeper. After a successful interview [13] with Mayfair hostess and businesswoman Dorothy Hartman, she had been appointed to her country house – the fourteenth century Stumblehole farm set in three-hundred acres in Surrey near Reigate; where she introduced a new alternative to English tea-time scones, Welshcakes.

The same summer we moved from our lodgings in Cardiff to a completely different world. I was not to see Tom again.

Tom's possessions had gradually been lost by the time he moved to Mag's as a lodger. His pre-war sheet music, once temporarily kept in Mag's piano stool had long been dispersed by various family clear outs.

So much family history is lost this way.

Duke Street viewed from the castle

New Theatre's 'Edwardian Baroque' Auditorium

The Hayes, David Morgan's department store on right

Post-war WNO poster

James Howell's department store St May's Street –where Tom worked as a store-keeper

them with mines. It began by a mining section formed from Welsh miners attached to the *Royal Engineers.*

In June they tunnelled under the Vimy Ridge in France and placed nearly one million tons of explosives. When it was exploded the noise was heard as far away as Dublin!

In June 1915 the Royal Engineers tunnelled under the Vimy Ridge in France

The same year, the Germans used gas in their attacks for the first time. The British responded during the *battle of Loos* in September.

The underground tunneller faced many threats: entombment, obliteration, health problems brought on by the workload, working environment and poor air quality; there was even the risk of drowning.

But the biggest killer was actually gas poisoning; not the designed toxic vapour variety used in cloud and shell form by troops on the surface, but carbon monoxide (CO), an invisible, odourless and tasteless substance, naturally produced by every explosive action – even the firing of a simple rifle bullet. In mines that broke the surface, or in the case of a shell burst, carbon monoxide quickly dissipated into the atmosphere.

However, after an underground explosion, it is trapped in the geology and tunnels. Despite this, the family remembers that Tom was ordered to return to these tunnels by un-sympathetic NCO's with consequential effects. Luckily for him the nursing care he received at *Hoogestadt hospital* helped his recovery, where Madame Curie and her daughter once briefly nursed. In October the same year English nurse Edith Cavell was not so lucky. She was shot at dawn by the Germans in Brussels for helping escaping prisoners.

Tom was now part of the *Royal Engineers* 255th Tunnelling Company, which was formed in January 1916. They moved to the middle of the Western Front in Flanders between Armentieres and Arras in what was known as the 'Red Lamp' to Neuve Chapelle sector.

In the same part of the front twelve months earlier, a certain Lieutenant Philip Neave had won a Victoria Cross. By strange co-incidence Tom was to meet and escape with him from Castello di Vincigliata, twenty years later during the next world war.

By early 1917 his Tunnelling Company was engaged in digging the subways to the front and constructing two 50,000-gallon underground water reservoirs, for the supply of forward troops in the Vimy attack of April 1917. He was finally billeted in the small town of Steenvoorde situated on the border with France and Belgium, when the war came to an end in November 1918.

Despite four years of war Tom had survived and was still only twenty. The fact he was alive at all was probably due to his tunnelling service with the *Royal Engineers* as opposed to the dreadful slaughter in the infantry battles. However, his life was a relentless existence beneath the Flanders fields, enduring physical and mental stresses in a complex war of silence, tension and claustrophobia.

Steenvoorde March 1918 - 255 Tunnelling Company Royal Engineers
Tom bottom row cross-legged – third from right (Author)

The experience he gained was to become invaluable for his many escape attempts in World War Two.

Before the war, he had left school in the winter of 1910, and worked with his father in the Merthyr Vale colliery. By the time he left for France four years later, Tom had two sisters, Margaret the eldest known as Mag, and Maudie, as well as four younger brothers, Arthur, Archie, George, Jess and Bernard. (Arthur also served in the army with the *Royal Welsh Fusiliers*).

It was a typical Welsh mining family home, many of whom sang in the church choir, always included a miner's caged canary, as well as a succession of Welsh terriers such as 'Nutty' and 'Boyo'. My mother

Lena Gwen, the last child and his youngest sister had yet to be born, arriving in September 1918 the same year as Winnie.

During the latter part of the Great War, whilst on leave Tom had met and fell for Violet -known as Vi, who was living locally. She was born in Suffolk in May 1900, the eldest daughter of Florence, and Thomas Tinsley. Born in Wales Thomas had once spent ten days in Swansea Gaol as a sixteen-year-old for stealing a bottle of whisky. Within a year the itinerant family had moved to Jubilee Terrace Ipswich where Thomas worked in a brewery, bottling mineral water.

Vi was remembered as *"a pretty seventeen years old, with long auburn hair."* It was said she was a nurse, possibly in the Voluntary Aid Detachment (VAD), who found herself pregnant as a result of an affair with a Canadian soldier.

Her daughter, named Winifred Muriel (known as Winnie) was born at 15 Brook Street, in the village of Blaenrhondda near Treherbert on March 15, 1918. On the birth certificate, Vi left the father details blank and described herself as a railway booking clerk.

Tom it seemed loved them both and they were welcomed into the Morgan family [15]. He unofficially adopted Winnie, and married her mother four years later in Merthyr registry office in February 1922, with Vi's father Thomas as witness. The twenty-one year old was then pregnant with his son Leslie, born on 3 July. They were living together at 48 Moy Road Aberfan, but for sake of propriety Tom gave his home address on the marriage certificate.

Left to Right: Cyril Woolley, Winnie and Vi with drinks in hand summer 1970 (kind permission Adrian Payne)

Winnie and Leslie c.1923-4 (Author)

Within a year or so the family moved to West Wales within the Afan Forest near Port Talbot; living at 4 Heol Treharne Abergwynfi, a twin village with Blaengwynfi where his sister Mag and family lived. Archie his youngest son was born there on 3 July 1924.

Soon after, Tom had left because of the coal recession and his health – choosing the open air. They moved to Cardiff and he became a painter, and then worked as a labourer in the timber trade.

After school, Winnie possibly encourage by her mother, trained as a nurse in London at *St Mary Abbot's Hospital* in the late 1920s early 1930s becoming a registered nurse in late 1933. [16]

Despite nursing demanding long hours (117 a fortnight), this was a wonderful achievement, because as many as 40% failed the examination. However, it seems an illness may have prevented her from practicing having developed pleurisy. She was sent to live with her widowed grandmother Florence Tinsley in Gloucestershire, in East Street Moreton in Marsh. It was thought the Cotswold air might improve her health.

By the late summer of 1937 the twenty-year-old, now a dressmaker had met and married Ralph a brickworks secretary, the youngest son of John and Ellen Payne. The wedding took place in St David's parish church Moreton in Marsh. Ralph recorded his father a baker, and Winnie declared her father a painter, both signed the register. They settled down in Northwick Terrace Blockley.

Just after war was declared, they had a son John; born on 23 September 1939 in *Morton & District Hospital*. Winnie was still there six days later when the Government Register was being compiled. John was Tom's first grandchild and the first 'great' grandchild in Tommy and Annie Morgan's wider family. At the outbreak of war Ralph served in the local Auxiliary Fire Service, and later they had another son Keith in 1944.

For many people in Britain the 1930s was a period of great hardship. The Wall Street Crash in 1929 started a worldwide economic depression that lasted for much of the decade. Old industries such as steel, ship-building and coal mining suffered the most. This affected Wales particularly, and the spectre of unemployment was always present. In 1936 the Spanish civil war had broken out and thousands of anti-fascists from Britain and particularly Wales went to Spain to fight alongside the loyal Spaniards and formed the British Battalion in the International Brigade. Out of the battalion's 170 Welsh volunteers, 116 were miners, one in five was married and the average age was over thirty. The South Wales miners provided the largest regional group.

Another Welshman, a single-minded 'cussed' sea captain appropriately named 'Potato' Jones in his tramp steamer *Marie Llewellyn,* persistently ran the Spanish blockade smuggling arms (and potatoes) to the beleaguered Republicans, often protected by the Royal Navy.

However it was not easy for volunteers, because under the Foreign Enlistment Act, they were breaking the law by joining the International Brigade. This legislation dated back to 1870 and was invoked because of a non-intervention agreement signed by 27 countries, including Britain. As a result, those who volunteered often went to great lengths to conceal their involvement. Tom could have used an alias, although I've found no records or remembered family stories about him volunteering for this war – which for many was a fight against Fascism.

Although Tom fitted the typical Welsh volunteer profile, he was more artistic than political (although some artist's volunteered like the writer and poet Lawrie Lee), and of course British intelligence kept a close eye on potential volunteers at the ports.

The Spanish Boy

A after the outbreak of the Spanish civil war and the bombing of Guernica in April 1937, an old steamship the *Habana* designed to carry 800, left the Basque port of Santurce near Bilbao in May, with nearly 4,000 children, teachers, helpers, catholic priests and two doctors headed for Southampton, over 200 found refuge in Wales.

This evacuation of children, reminds me of an earlier family story about a young dispossessed Spanish boy wandering Cardiff docks much earlier around 1900 –at the time one of the largest docks in the world with seven miles of quaysides.

The boy was found apparently lost, wandering alone one wet night along the quayside, by Josiah Morgan who was a Dock Pilot at that time. The story goes that he was taken home to the family house in Telford Street, and perhaps temporarily adopted. No name or records emerge –not unusual for the times but this event tallies with historical facts.

The *Orconero Iron Ore Company* in the Basque region of northern Spain had been a subsidiary of the *Dowlais Iron Company* in South Wales since 1873. In 1900 several hundred Spanish workers and their families were brought from Bilbao by sea to Cardiff Bute docks and then by rail to Dowlais, in what were seen as a way of undercutting wages for Welsh workers. The scheme back-fired, the Spanish quickly integrated and joined the union. They built single story houses in Dowlais, King Alphonso Street (today just Alphonso Street) named after the Spanish monarch of the time. Some areas of Georgetown and Penywern were given over to them, creating the largest Spanish community in Britain. One hopes the 'Spanish boy' was re-united with his family.

At the beginning of 1939, six years after retiring, the health of Tom's father had deteriorated with the miner's 'black lung disease' (pneumoconiosis) and he died on Thursday 20 April a few weeks after his sixty-sixth birthday. It would be the last time that all the (grown-up) Morgan children, Tom's brothers and sisters gathered together in the family home in Merthyr Vale, a few months before the beginning of the Second World War.

Although historically rural Wales was traditionally a matriarchal society; Welsh funerals were particularly singular back then, it was only men that attended them, regardless of whether man or woman had died. Immediately, on a death, curtains were drawn in the house and, out of sympathy, in all the adjoining houses in the street. It was reported in the press, as the Morgan's were held in high regard within the tight mining community of Merthyr Vale and Aberfan and many remember it one of the largest funeral processions before war broke out.

The house in Station Terrace would have been full of family and relatives visiting with their condolences. All Tommy Morgan's grandchildren attended, Leslie and Archie (Tom's sons), Don (Mag's son), and Raymond (Arthur's son).

That following Tuesday 'Tommy' Morgan was buried in the Aberfan cemetery arranged by local undertakers Messrs. D & S Rees, of Brookfield with the Reverends' Nicholls and Millward assisting. During the all-male procession from the house to the graveside a mile or so away, the communal hymn singing creating that collective sound, a spiritual and emotional experience as only the Welsh seem to achieve.

Tom's father's funeral gathering 1939 - the nine Morgan children
Left to Right: Jess, Bernard, Gwen (author's mother), Maudie, George, Mag, Arthur, Archie, Tom (Author)

Gwen (19) and Leslie (15) Morgan August 1937 (author)

Tom's sons Leslie (17) and Archie (15) at the same funeral 1939 (Author)

Another war

Tom was forty-one in February 1939, and once again the prospect of a war with Germany loomed. The same year the first Anderson Shelter was built in London, Britain pledged support to Poland in the event of an invasion and the Military Training Act was passed by Parliament.

Winnie had settled in the Cotswolds, Leslie had left leaving only Archie now fifteen in the family home. Tom's tempestuous marriage to Vi was probably in terminal decline, his family responsibilities largely over. In September [17] he was living at 8 Clyde Street, Adamsdown Cardiff with Vi listed as 'unpaid domestic duties', two other lodgers and his younger brother Bernard –both he and Tom employed as Heavy Timber Porters.

A year later Bernard had married twenty-seven year old Morfydd Jones in Cardiff and their son Brian was born in Clyde Street in August 1940. However friction developed between Vi and Morfydd [18] and she felt compelled to return with her baby to her family village of Aberfan taking rented rooms in Angus Street.

Tom gives his year of birth as 1899 –making him (officially) a year younger. One can only imagine certain restlessness, a chance now war had been declared, to seek adventure and join the Army again.

Tom's eldest son Leslie, remembered as *"a tall, good looking boy"* a younger contemporary of my mother, was seventeen when war broke out, and eventually called up –joining the army like his father.

I believe he was posted to the Far East in 1941. He may have had had a flair for languages which gained him a commission as a 2nd Lieutenant in the British Indian Army. He too would survive the war.

Two more of Annie Morgan's 'boys' Jess and Bernard also served in the forces during the Second World War. The others, Arthur, Archie and George were either too old or in reserved occupations.

She also had three young grandsons fighting; Don Rees serving in the RAF, his brother Russ and Leslie Morgan in the army. In addition, she had two of her son-in-law's Jack Prichard and Jack Dann both in the Royal Navy.

Bernard joined the 1st Battalion of the *Welch Regiment*, as a private soldier taking part in *Operation Husky* the Allied invasion of Sicily in July 1943, and the following Italian campaigns. He was wounded in September 1944 during the bitter battles around Monte Croce near San Marino. The regiment had been severely mauled and reduced, but when it reformed towards 1945, the *Welch* had managed to fight their way to the Yugoslav frontier.

Rest Bay, Porthcawl, c.1935
Left to Right: Bernard (youngest son), Tommy and Annie Morgan, Lea Morgan (eldest daughter of brother George), Tom (eldest son)

Tom in 'heroic' pose c.1939
(images Author)

Jess had joined the army pre-war as a career soldier and served in India, returning to England before the war. With the rank of corporal he took part in the *BEF -British Expeditionary Force* to France and the subsequent retreat to Dunkirk in the summer of 1940. After officers had deserted them, he brought all the men from his company safely back to England. This initiative was immediately rewarded with a commission. As Captain Morgan, he later served in *Royal Pioneer Corps*; (like Tom) attached to the East Africa Command in the northern rail-head town of Kitale in the Rift valley.

With the exception of Jack Dann, they all survived the war. Bernard returned to mining, and Jess became a sub-post master in Essex.

-5-

To war, again

Second World War

"Then it's Tommy this, an' Tommy that,
An' Tommy 'ow's yer soul?
But it's thin red line of 'eroes,
When the drums begin to roll."

'Tommy', Rudyard Kipling

For this war he was officially 'too old', but in typical Tom fashion had put his age down to enlist in the Army. His previous experience gained him quick promotion and he achieved the rank of Company Quarter-Master Sergeant. And so, CQMS [19] T H Morgan Number 13037936 joined the newly formed *Royal Pioneer Corps* a combatant corps used for light engineering tasks. He was attached to the Base Depot, Middle East Forces and went to war for the second time. They sailed to Egypt in 1941 taking the circuitous route in a WS convoy (Winston's specials) round Africa via the Cape.

The war in the Mediterranean and North Africa initially went well for Britain, at sea the Royal Navy had disabled much of the Italian fleet, and our Army had driven the Italians out of Cyrenaica into Tripolitania. This began to change when the Germans re-enforced them and a certain German General Erwin Rommel began to make his mark.

'Tommy – for you the war is over'

The port of Tobruk in Italian controlled Cyrenaica (North East Libya) on the Mediterranean Sea was a fiercely contested objective. It was first taken by the British in January 1941. A few months later in March and April the Germans counter-attacked under Erwin Rommel and drove them out, leaving the Australian garrison at Tobruk isolated.

However, the garrison was provisioned by sea and withstood repeated German attacks. The next British counter-attack under Field Marshal Claude Auchinleck in December 1941 relieved the siege. Both sides then paused to regroup and strengthen their forces.

In May 1942, Rommel again renewed his offensive, but was initially blocked by strong resistance and caught between two strong-points on the defensive Gazala Line.

Tobruk was thought to be a stronghold with a mixed contingent of South African, Indian, Ghurkhas and the *Coldstream Guards* Brigade. However, living up to his nickname of the 'Desert Fox', Rommel wheeled his Panzer tanks through the desert smashing the defenders of Bir Hacheim, and taking Tobruk on 17 June.

He captured 30,000 defenders including CQMS Morgan, as well as the supply dump there. Tom's capture was a huge disappointment as he was due for leave and would have returned to Cairo to receive his Commission. Thus captured he remained a Company Quarter-Master Sergeant for the rest of the war. Tobruk was retaken by the British some months later, but by this time he was a prisoner of war.

On different sides: Uncle Tom and Rommel at the capture of Tobruk North Africa in 1942. Tom was denied his commission and became a POW – but Rommel was promoted Field-Marshall. To the victor the spoils!

The Germans handed their prisoners over to the Italians who transported them by sea to Italy. He was taken to *Campo P.G. 78* at Sulmona, a prisoner of war camp located in Abruzzo, East of Rome. It served as a prisoner of war camp in both world wars. It was home to as many as 3,000 British and Commonwealth officers and other ranks captured in North Africa.

The camp itself was built on a hillside and consisted of a number of brick barracks surrounded by a high wall. However, the captured officers fared much better being allocated to the Villa Orsini nearby, surrounded by gardens with views to the mountain range to the East. As one captured officer, Carton de Wiart describes in his book:

"......from our villa we could see a hotel, high up in the mountain perched like an eagle's nest. It was known as Terminillo. Later it became famous for the sensational rescue by air of Mussolini by Germans, after he had been imprisoned by his own people." [20]

This daring attack took place on Sunday morning 12 September 1943, led by SS Officer Otto Skorzeny with a German special-forces unit of ninety parachutists in a glider-borne rescue, landing on the Gran Sasso Mountains near the hotel taking the guards by surprise.

After some time in Sulmona, Tom was later moved by train northward towards Florence to another prisoner of war camp, this time a requisitioned 'Englishman's' castle.

Castello di Vincigliata –Campo 12

The thirteenth century castle located near Florence on a hill close to Fiesole is Medieval in origin, once the ancient stronghold of the *Visdomini* Family. It was reconstructed by the Englishman Sir John Temple Leader in the 1850s. In the course of fifteen years he rebuilt the castle in the neo-gothic style from the ground up. It was a romantic vision of a feudal fortress.

He also bought the surrounding land, more than seven-hundred acres in the space of fifty years, began the delicate task of reclaiming it, restoring the houses and villas, creating the *Bosco di Vincigliata*, planting cypresses in the rocky areas where nothing else would grow, pines, and all the various shrubs and bushes one finds in a typical Central Italian woodland, in short, an English Romantic Garden on a huge scale.

People flocked from afar to visit his castle and admire the grounds, and he was extremely pleased when the *Illustrated London News* printed an engraving of Queen Victoria doing a watercolour of the *Giardino delle Colonne,* a pretty pool fed by the Mensola creek, during her visit in 1893. Sir John married late in life and died without heirs.

The property passed to a nephew who sold it off piecemeal, and his art collection was scattered. It then went through a series of hands, with the castle being used by the Italian Government as a prison for English officers during World War Two.

Castello di Vincigliata near Florence, taken by Lt-General Neame in 1946
The tunnel was driven between Sept. 1942 and Mar. 1943 under the keep, driveway and outer wall

It was to this castle, now designated *P.G. 12* Vincigliata –a camp for distinguished military prisoners that Tom arrived after his incarceration at Sulmona. Vincigliata was much smaller containing no more than around twenty five prisoners, including Non-Commissioned officers some other ranks and a dozen or so officers.

He found himself in impressive military company. Amongst his fellow inmates included Major-General Sir Adrian Carton de Wiart, Air-Marshal Owen Boyd, Lieutenant-General Richard O'Connor, Lieutenant General Philip Neame, Major-General Michael Gambier-Parry, and New Zealander Brigadiers Reginald Miles and James Hargest.

Most were captured in North Africa during various phases of the war, although Air-Marshall Boyd was captured in Sicily when his bomber aircraft had to make a forced landing. They were carrying £250,000 destined for Malta, which had to be quickly ditched in the Mediterranean. His pilot Flight-Lieutenant John Leeming was later to succeed repatriation to Britain by feigning madness. [21]

O'Connor had been the brilliant commander of 7th Armoured Division and 4th Indian Brigade that earlier in the North African campaign had routed the Italian 10th army taking surrender of 130,000 men and 400 tanks. Unfortunately, he was captured with Lt-General Neame by a German reconnaissance night patrol in April 1941, during their retreat from Benghazi.

Neame, won the Victoria Cross during the First World War in December 1914 at Neuve Chapelle when, as a twenty-six-year-old *Royal Engineers* lieutenant, in the face of heavy fire engaged the Germans in a single-handed bombing attack and rescued many wounded. (Coincidentally, Tom also served in the RE's as teenage private in the same sector, later in the war).

Ten years later Neame won a gold medal for shooting at the 1924 Paris Olympics -the only VC to win an Olympic medal. In these games Britain won nine gold medals, including Harold Abrahams in the 100 metres and Eric Liddell in the 400, both athletes memorably celebrated in the 1981 film *Chariots of Fire*. Philip Neame was the nephew of a founding father of the Kent-based *Shepherd Neame* brewing dynasty, the oldest in Kent.

Carton de Wiart, from a well-connected Continental family, was appointed by Churchill as Head of a Military Mission en-route to Yugoslavia. He was captured when his Wellington aircraft from Malta crash-landed in the sea off the coast of North Africa in April 1941. He too had won a VC in the First World War, on the Somme, wounded eight times, losing a hand and eye.

He was the alleged model for the fictional flamboyant Brigadier Ritchie-Hook in Evelyn Waugh's post-war *Sword of Honour* trilogy.

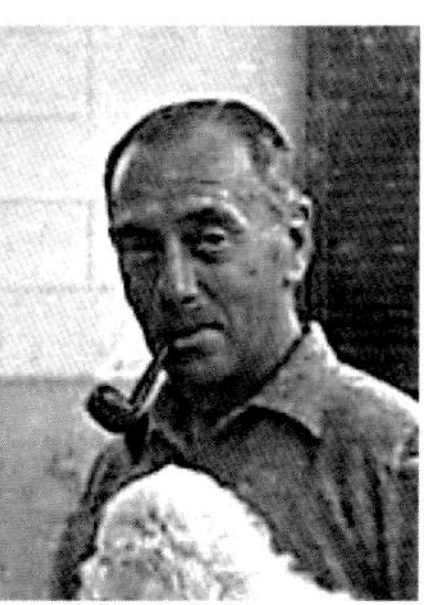

Some officers imprisoned in Castello di Vincigliata 1941 -43
Left to Right: Major-General Sir Adrian Carton de Wiart, Lt-General Sir Richard O'Connor, Lt-General Philip Neame, Major-General Michael Gambier-Parry (camp forger)
Tom escaped with O'Connor and Neame after the Italian armistice in September 1943.

Amongst the many clandestine British secret services during World War Two was a department known as MI9. It worked to train the armed forces in escape and evasion. Evasion lines were set up in occupied countries. MI9 exchanged coded letters with prisoner of war camps, and secretively sent in money, maps, clothes and many other useful tools. What the Italians never knew that O'Connor had one of their codes and was therefore secretively in touch with London.

The officers were separated from the non-commissioned officers and the only link between them was via the officers 'batmen' or servants who attended them. Tom was the senior Non-Commissioned Officer, NCO, and sang in the choir at church service on Sundays, conducted by Major-General Michael Gambier-Parry. GP as he was known, had been *Aide-de-Camp* to the King and had won a Military Cross in the first world war, as Carton de Wiart wryly observed, *"...he was also a most gifted man, made delightful sketches, was a first class 'forger' – which could no doubt earn him a steady income in the underworld."* [22]

The Gambier-Parry's, were an artistic and military family. His father was a renowned church architect, and his half-brother Sir Hubert Parry the eminent composer of *Jerusalem.* His younger brother Richard was serving in communications with Military intelligence -MI6.

After the war Tom had explained to mum that via these secret MI9 instructions [23] only officers were to make the escape. NCOs and other ranks were ordered to do everything to help them – except make their own escape!

This must have been a very frustrating order to obey. There were a number of escape plans from the castle as most of the officers had been there about a year before Tom arrived. These had failed with the inevitable punishment of a month's solitary confinement.

Then in mid-September 1942 a tunnel was started and designed by Neame. Various officers took it in turns to work on it in shifts of four hours per day. This was hard blistering work, but they managed to successfully evade detection, over the next six months.

It was completed by 20 March 1943. The plan was for six selected officers to escape in pairs; O'Connor with Carton de Wiart, Combe with Boyd and the two New Zealanders Hargest and Miles together. Waiting for the right conditions they eventually escaped on the evening of 29 March.

Neame in his book pays tribute to the support he and fellow officers received from fellow POW's:

"*...while the remaining six officers and thirteen NCOs and men went through hours of tedious watching to ensure success. Every one, officers and men, were in it, and wildly keen for success!*" [24]

The escape proceeded brilliantly with all officers escaping remaining undetected until the following day, enough time for the escapees to be far away.

They all had their adventures which have been described in their books. O'Connor and Carton de Wiart (who was now aged sixty-three) were captured in the region of the Bologna in the Po Valley, after eight days, while Combe was caught at Milan railway station. Boyd managed to board a train and reach Como before he too was apprehended. However the New Zealanders, Reg Miles and James Hargest secured their escape by journeying by rail and then walking over the border into Switzerland.

Neame received a coded letter from Miles two weeks later confirming their safe arrival.

As a punishment, after the discovery of the tunnel all the officers' batmen were transferred to another camp. Eventually the four captured officers were returned to the camp for thirty days solitary. As Carton de Wiart reflects in his book:

"*....I learnt also that twenty-four hours elapsed before our exit hole had been discovered, and then only by Gussie's dog (Mickey). Gussie (as Lieutenant Agosto Ricciardi their previous Italian guard and Gaoler was known) had left it behind when he had been sent away, but the dog proved too intimate a friend to us, and had unwittingly given away our secret.*" [25]

A new camp Commander was appointed and the garrison was increased by fifty-percent - there were now some hundred infantry and *carabinieri* to guard eleven officers and fourteen NCO's and other ranks. The final and successful escape was not made until after the Italian surrender in September 1943.

However, in the preceding months, the inmates of the castle had through MI9 continued to receive parcels with much concealed escape material including over 20,000 lire currency, various maps, compasses and some clothing material.

Italy

CAMPO P.G. 12 P.M. 3200
VINCIGLIATA

Thirteen senior British officers and 13 orderlies are detained in a villa here near Florence. The villa is described as being like a country house, with beautiful views of the city and the neighbouring hills.

The officers spend much of their time working in the gardens. The promised visit by a C. of E. chaplain to the camp at Christmas, unfortunately, did not take place. It was hoped that the chaplain from Lucca Hospital would be able to visit the camp at Easter. *(Visited*

The Red Cross sent a delegation to Campo 12 in March. Their bland report appeared in the June edition of '*Prisoner of War*' magazine, including an image of some (un-named) British prisoners appearing relaxed on the castle battlements. *(Above image: extreme left, possibly Tom?)*

After the elation of the escape Tom received sad news from home about my father death, his ship *HMS Lightning* had been sunk two months earlier. He responded to his youngest sister with a short POW postal card dated 21 May 1943.

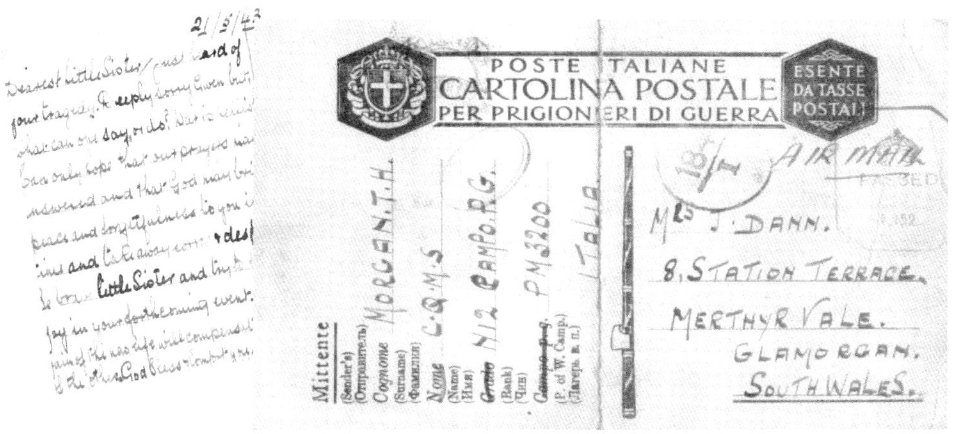

"Dearest Little Sister / just heard of your tragedy. Deeply sorry Gwen but, what can I say or do? War is hellish. Can only hope that our prayers may be answered and that God may bring peace and forgetfulness to you in time and take away sorrow and despair. Be brave little sister and try and to find joy in your forthcoming event. The gain of the new life will compensate for the loss of the other. God bless and comfort you. xxxxx Tom, Love to Mam"

Then in mid-August Carton de Wiart was selected by the Italians as part of their proposed armistice negotiations with the allies. He was a friend of the Italian Crown Princess (Marie José of Belgium, married to King Umberto II) and they hoped this connection would help.

He was taken to Rome and met with the Italian Deputy Chief of Staff General Zanussi, after a few days they travelled on to neutral Lisbon. By the end of the month he was flown to England a free man.

Once the press announced his arrival in England he received many letters from relations of prisoners asking for news. His reply quoted in his memoirs gives a glimpse of his terse style and may explain Toms' views of him.

"The chief inconvenience (sic) was the letters I received in their hundreds, many from relations and friends of prisoners in Italy asking for news which I could not give, as I had none!" [26]

Then on 8 September 1943, the Captain in charge of Castello di Vincigliata announced that the Italian government had arranged an armistice.

At nine in the morning two days later all the remaining prisoners of war were sent to Florence as the Germans were approaching. General Chiappe, a sympathetic Italian officer arranged a special train, taking them to Arezzo some sixty miles south. Using the smuggled Lire they bought various civilian clothes from local Italians at Campo di Marte railway station. Suitably attired Neame, O'Connor, (who had learnt Italian whilst in prison) with eleven officers together with fourteen other ranks including CQMS Morgan set off to evade capture.

After arriving in Arezzo they discovered much confusion and a general air of despondency with many Italian officials. So the officers decided it was safer to move away the same evening with all the escaping soldiers. They travelled some forty miles northward to the Hospice of Camadoli in the Apennine Mountains. They stayed four days.

Some officers climbed another thousand feet higher to the Monastery in Eremo where the Prior-General of the Camaldolese Order resided. He was pro-British – hated the fascists and detailed one of the brothers Don Leoni to act as special liaison between the British escaped Prisoners. Links with MI9 were re-established and money provided to help with food and shelter in an already impoverished Italian countryside.

After the Italian armistice there was much concern in the British press as to what would happen with the British prisoners held in Italy. So it was some comfort in Wales that Tom was reported safe; relayed from the Vatican by Father Patrick Lenane the parish priest of Saint Benedict's church in Merthyr Vale, from his presbytery on Cardiff Road.

Italy was still politically divided and word reached the Prior-General that an Italian fascist had betrayed their presence. For their safety the escaping prisoners were led from the Monastery to hide and live amongst the Italians mostly in the mountain villages of Segeteina and Strabatenza some ten miles away.

In September and October the soldiers helped the peasants with their manual work such as digging, fetching water and husking maize.

O'Connor or Neame would make regular visits to check on the soldiers' welfare and give them any news. During this time Neame and O'Connor had collected another twenty or so British soldiers who had also escaped after the armistice and were wandering the mountains.

As a precaution the officers built brushwood hides in the surrounding woods, to sleep overnight as there were frequent alarms about spies and impending searches. Then on the morning of 29 October, 120 Germans arrived by motor Lorries and surrounded the village to search it. They had again been betrayed. The approaching Germans were seen by the officers from higher up the mountains and with help from one of the guides in the village escaped. [27]

The other soldiers in Segeteina including Tom were not so lucky. After seven weeks of freedom they were again prisoners of war – this time by the Germans. Tom later told my mother that he remembered with much sadness seeing the elderly Italian woman who had sheltered and looked after him in the village being taken away by the Germans – probably to be shot. He had a very high regard for all Italian women he met, and thought them brave and strong.

Stalag VIIA

After his recapture in Italy* he was transported to a transit camp in the Po valley and onward to Germany by train. Sixty prisoners were crammed into each boxcar as the train made its way slowly over the Brenner Pass through the Austrian borders to Munich and Stalag VIIA. This German prisoner of war camp was located just outside Moosburg in southern Bavaria about twenty two miles North East of Munich. Originally planned to hold 10,000 prisoners, but at the time of its liberation there were about 80,000 prisoners from at least twenty-six nations on the camp roster.

* Tom's Italian POW records list *Camp 82 Laterina* near Arezzo –not *Camp 12 Vincigliata*, an understandable mistake perhaps as it shared the same postal number. Many British prisoners re-captured came from *Camp 82*, hiding in that same Italian village after the armistice. Alternatively Tom may have deliberately misled the authorities to avoid interrogation about the high ranking prisoners at *Campo 12.*

Welcome to Stalag VIIA

Meal distribution

The first American arrivals came after the Tunisian and Italian Campaigns during 1942-3. Amongst the last arrivals in January 1945 were officers from *Stalag Luft III* (scene of the 'Great Escape') who had been force-marched from Sagan in Silesia.

It was the largest prisoner of war camp in Germany covering 86 acres. For prisoners sleeping in two tier bunks, in cramped conditions in a hut with thirty men, where food was scarce, with no one wanting to be there, meant there were some tense times. It was the practice of the British prisoners, (to the amazement of other nationals) to throw open all the windows at night to let the air circulate in the hut, no matter what the weather!

Stalag VIIA main watchtower overlooking British soldiers

inside a typical hut

During this time Tom had been involved in many escape attempts already, and had suffered beatings for them. As usual he would have been placed on bread and water in the 'Sonderbarracke', an area just inside the main gate a special detention jail for POWs who had tried to escape. Tom's strength of character shines through, even after the failed escape attempts his spirit would not be broken, although the mental and physical scars would remain. This is where music and singing would play it healing part after the war.

By the time Captain D. W. D. Bond, *Grenadier Guards* arrived in Moosburg in September 1944; CQMS Thomas Morgan had been there for about ten months.

Bond had been captured in Italy –not far from Vincigliata. He had been with others in a jeep on the south side of the river Arno in

Florence, close to the front line - but believing the Germans had withdrawn. So on a sunny afternoon *"after a good lunch"* he drove into a road block thinking it was the British forward position –it wasn't. It was a German Wehrmacht Parachutist Battalion and he was taken prisoner.

In his book written years after the war, Bond still recalled two vivid incidents whilst at Stalag VIIA related to Tom as follows:

The tunnel

"The entrance to the tunnel was from under the last seat on the left in the latrine and it was strictly taboo to use it. One day a Greek Officer who believed in squatting on top of the seat in the Greek manner absent-mindedly arranged himself on the forbidden seat only to be impaled in the arse on a home-made entrenching tool wielded by a furious Welsh tunneller [Tom Morgan] who caught him just in time.
Sadly for the POWs who had been digging away for months the tunnel ended in disaster. One sunny day, when the entire population of the compound was walking round the exercise area, or playing football, one of the large telegraph poles carrying the perimeter lighting slowly and gracefully sank into the ground. The tunnel had gone right underneath it. The Germans went berserk. They rushed into the compound with guard dogs barking and yelping." [28]

The dog

"The dogs were not always as frightening as they seemed….on one occasion we saw an extraordinary incident take place in the NCOs compound which was next to ours on the other side from the Russian Officers. It was during an air raid. As soon as the air-raid siren sounded all prisoners were supposed to return to their huts immediately. On this particular day a sergeant was just bringing the water for his tea to the boil on his stoofah (a personal smokeless cooker made out of old Red Cross tins) when the siren went. Nothing was going to move him.

He quietly ignored the guards' shouts of 'Raus Raus!' and stubbornly went on feeding in the fuel and cranking the handle. The guards didn't like it! They released a dog towards him. It charged across the compound with fangs bared and barking hysterically. We watched in horror as it reached the sergeant. The dog stopped. Its barking turned to a friendly whine and it fawned against him and licked his face. The Germans went mad. Two guards rushed over, kicked the sergeant, kicked the dog harder, smashed the stoofah and dragged the sergeant away – still kicking the dog in a frenzy of rage." [29]

The following day a notice went up in all huts:

"IT HAS COME TO THE NOTICE
THAT GUARD DOGS OF THE RED CROSS PARCELS
HAVE BEEN FED!
THIS PRACTICE WILL CEASE!!
THE DOGS WILL NOT ACCEPT THESE RATIONS!!!" [30]

These memories and other experiences were to be relived and celebrated again by Captain Bond and CQMS Morgan –the Welsh tunneller' and 'brave Sergeant' - in a Cardiff pub ten years later.

The camp was liberated by General Patton's 7th US Army on 29 April 1945, and Bond describes the moment,

"After a bit an American Jeep and a Sherman tank moved slowly down the Lagerstrasse. You could hardly see the tank for prisoners climbing all over it. Nearly all the 100,000 prisoners were crying, but not so much as the tank crew who had tears pouring down their cheeks. We did not realise how thin and strained we all looked and our appearance must have been a shock to our liberators." [31]

I remember mum repeating many times that despite being liberated by the American's Tom had little time for them. Largely based on their tendency to brag, coupled with (in his view) their poor military resolve and discipline. No doubt reflecting on his experiences in Stalag VIIA – as it housed the largest concentration of Americans of any prisoner of war camp.

Typically when the daily Appell (parade) was called British soldiers turned out as smart as possible maintaining their standards of drill, keeping self-respect and morale and in turn the respect of the enemy. The Americans, on the other hand, would often turn out unshaven, scruffy and with hands in their pockets. As Bond reflects in his memoirs *"They looked like a defeated army –we did not."*

Moment of surrender: Stalag VIIA April 1945
The Sherman tank is invisible covered in welcoming POW's

(Left) Deputy camp commandant Maj. Gustav Simoliet,
(Centre) Lt. Col. James W Lamm, US 47th Tank Battalion,
(Right) Group Captain Kellett, RAF, Senior British Officer

After the end of hostilities in Europe, orders were given to repatriated prisoners of war in *Operation Exodus*. Throughout May thousands of allied prisoners of war were ferried to England with arrangements made for their reception at *RAF Oakley*, Buckinghamshire, with refreshments laid on in the social club.

Operation Exodus 1945 – 'Blighty and Cardiff' chalked on fuselage!

The RAF and the USAF made available a range of aircraft including Dakotas as well as bombers like the Lancaster's, Halifax's, Stirling's, and Boeing B-17 Flying Fortresses.

Within a few days former prisoners were flown by the Americans in Dakota aircraft from the local airfield at Landshut to Lille in Northern France, where they were fed deloused and stayed overnight in a specially prepared 'tented town'.

The following day Tom was ferried by air in a RAF Lancaster bomber to England –the pilot taking a route low over the white cliffs of Dover –as an emotional welcome home.

They were met by a reception committee made up of various women's services WVS, WRNS, ATS and WAAFs, -rows of trestle tables with English tea of paste and cucumber sandwiches, home-made cakes, with real tea, milk and sugar whilst they waited for transport to transit centres.

After a de-briefing he was fitted out with a new uniform, ration card, travel warrant and some cash. Telegrams were sent to family advising his arrival in England.

He was now free to make his way home.

-6-

A blackbird sang

Giorni della merla – "Close by, and round him…"

For Tom the war was finally over – he had his forty-seventh birthday in Stalag VIIA; he'd been a prisoner of war for nearly three years and away from home for five.

He travelled to Wales and was met at Cardiff General (now Central) Station by his wife Vi who blithely announced in her vitriolic way, *"your mother died four days ago (2nd May) and I'm divorcing you."* [32]

Despite the obvious lack of empathy with her husband, ironically it was to Tom's mother Annie Morgan she sort comfort and advice during his war-time imprisonment, and during the uncertainty of his whereabouts in the confusion of the Italian armistice.

After the war, sometime in the late 1940s it was rumoured that Vi was now living with a certain Mr Woolley.

Tom continued his journey a further nineteen miles as the Great Western Railway's branch train wound its way up the old Taff Vale line to Merthyr Vale station. He walked the last few hundred yards towards his old family home at 8 Station Terrace.

His 'mam' did not live to see 'her boys come home'. It was a sad homecoming, the only family to greet him was his widowed youngest sister Gwen and her twenty two month old son – me; but at least he was able to kiss away each hour of *Hiraeth.*

Home again, he was to live another twelve years enjoying music and singing with the fledgling Welsh National Opera Company.

A fitting tribute to his original composition, are the lyrics of *We'll Keep a Welcome,* as it captures Tom's musical score perfectly – because we now know who 'really' wrote the music don't we?

"Far away a voice is calling
Bells of memory chime
Come home again, come home again
They call through the oceans of time
We'll keep a welcome in the hillside
We'll keep a welcome in the Vales
This land you knew will still be singing
When you come home again to Wales
This land of song will keep a welcome
And with a love that never fails
We'll kiss away each hour of Hiraeth
When you come home again to Wales"

Not far from Blockley, is the station of Moreton in Marsh where the Cotswold railway line once linked another village station (now closed) called Adlestrop about five miles away.

Adlestrop, the name was immortalised by Edward Thomas in his poem, published a few weeks after his death in action during the *Battle of Arras* in 1917.

The Anglo-Welsh poet had been travelling by train some years earlier, when it made an unscheduled stop. His notes for the poem describe a moment of calm pause in which he remembers:

"…The steam hissed. Someone cleared his throat.
No one left and no one came
On the bare platform. What I saw
Was Adlestrop -- only the name

And willows, willow-herb, and grass,
And meadowsweet, and haycocks dry,
No whit less still and lonely fair
Than the high cloudlets in the sky"

"And for that minute a blackbird sang.
Close by, and round him, mistier,
Farther and farther, all the birds
Of Oxfordshire and Gloucestershire"

Winnie and Ralph in later years

Interior of St Peter & St Paul

Blockley village High Street c.1950s

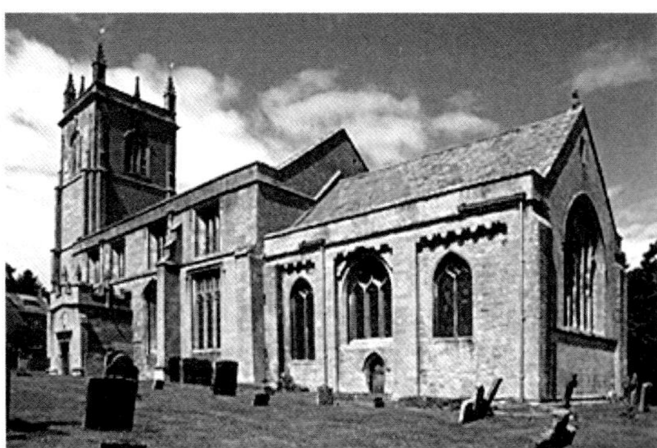

The approach and churchyard c.1950s

After a service attended by his close family and friends Tom was buried in the twelfth century churchyard of St Peter & St Paul's [33] Blockley, Gloucestershire in the spring of 1957, with our farewell wreath full of primroses, and I would like to think, a blackbird sang!

-7-

Postscripts

"History with its flickering lamp stumbles along the trail of the past, trying to reconstruct its scenes, to revive its echoes",...

Winston Churchill November 1940

Not one of the various military memoirs listed in this story, mention CQMS Tom Morgan by name, despite playing his part he has been air-brushed out of history. Only references to anonymous rank or obliquely such as "*that brave Sergeant*" linger on and of course his musical legacy has been reassigned. Even some of his war records are elusive.

However the reader will now know something of his life and this short memoir serves as my tribute.

Castello di Vincigliata June 2011: the author in the rose garden - with an unchanged view towards Florence, the Basilica di Santa Maria del Fiore (Il Duomo di Firenze) seen in distance -far right

Whilst on holiday in the summer of 2011 I visited Castello di Vincigliata, a twenty minute taxi ride from Florence. I was met by a young family member. She showed me around, explaining the present owners offer the castle as a venue for weddings, gala dinners and wine tasting events; it was used by *BBC TV's MasterChef* programme in 2013. Its vineyard the Testamatta Estate is run by Bibi Graetz a highly acclaimed wine-maker and artist, who designed his own labels. He produces the indigenous varieties of *Sangiovese, Canaiolo* and *Colorino.*

She offered an estate *Soffocone* at the end of my visit, only to have the offer promptly withdrawn by the owner, her parsimonious uncle, –as it retails at something like £70 a bottle!

All accounts of life at *Campo 12 - Castello di Vincigliata* are interesting but the most detailed was written by Lt-Gen. Sir Philip Neame secretly at the time. It was smuggled out and hidden in the Monastery at Eremo (often visited by St Francis in the thirteenth century) by the Prior-General of the Camaldolese Order. Subsequently it was retrieved by a British SOE agent in November 1944. Both he and

O'Connor arrived safely to England in December 1943. He retired after the war becoming Lieutenant-Governor of Guernsey, and died in 1978. He was I believe, what Tom might have called a 'soldiers' soldier.

Neame's aide-de-camp Lt. Dan Ranfurly (Sixth Earl of Ranfurly) also escaped and his time with the partisans features in the published wartime diaries of his equally adventurous wife, Hermione.

Flt. Lt. John Leeming wrote a humorous and amusing account, of his incarceration, cumulating with his escape by feinting madness. Cleverly planned over months –he was finally repatriated from Lucca hospital by train to neutral Lisbon then by hospital ship to England.

Brigadier Hargest a New Zealander was the only officer to escape successfully through the castle tunnel. He initially escaped with fellow New Zealander Brigadier Miles, who in a fit of depression close to the Spanish frontier inexplicably shot himself. Hargest continued alone arriving in England in November 1943. He became the highest-ranking British officer to escape in either war. He was killed in Normandy in August 1944.

Major-General Gambier-Parry escaped after the Italian armistice, smuggled to Rome by partisans early in 1944. He initially obtained sanctuary in a secret room within Signora Di Rienzo's fourth-floor apartment in the Via Ruggero Bonghi. Later he was hidden in a hospital on Via Santo Stefano Rotundo run by the Little Sisters of Mary; all arranged by an Irish priest known as the 'Vatican Pimpernel' [34] 'under the noses' of the Germans until the allies arrived in June. He retired soon after, becoming Deputy Lieutenant of Wiltshire, and died in 1976.

Lt-Gen. Sir Carton De Wiart's autobiography published in 1950 (Churchill penned the forward), was a remarkable military memoir with glimpses of his terse and flamboyant personality. Undoubtedly he was an extremely brave, if slightly brusque and eccentric officer – in the mould of 'they-don't-make-them-like-that-anymore'. He retired from the Army after the war and died in Ireland in 1963. He was one of Churchill's favourites but probably not one of Tom's!

The actor Derek Bond was in his late thirties at the time of the Cardiff reunion with Tom, and leading parts were beginning to elude him. In the 1960s he turned to television where he was co-presenter of *Picture Parade* for more than two years before joining *Tonight* a current-affairs programme. Of his dramatic roles on television, he was a creditable intelligence chief (1969) in *Callan*, a long-running thriller series starring Edward Woodward. He was married three times, and published his wartime memoirs over forty years later, written in an urbane and amusing style, with oblique references to Tom. He died in London October 2006, aged eighty-six.

Winnie and Ralph continued to live in Blockley, had two sons, and later moved to School Road Hampton in Evesham. One assumes any animosity between Vi and Winnie had been healed by 1970 as a photo shows them smiling and relaxing socially.

Winnie died in 1983 aged sixty-five. Ralph a retired surveyor some ten year older, died in 1995 aged eighty-seven. They are both buried in the fourteenth century parish churchyard of St Andrew's Hampton.

Tom's estranged wife 'Vi' never did divorce him. During the war she had met a married man Cyril Woolley in Cardiff; who was an accounts clerk in the Air Ministry. Woolley was born in Romford, as a young man had moved to Cardiff where he met Lillian Thomas. Both in their early twenties, they married in the autumn of 1924. They had a daughter in 1927 and by the summer of 1939 were living in Boverton Street, Roath Park.

After Tom's death Vi moved to South East London. She lived with her gentleman friend Woolley and son Leslie. From around 1958 to 1964 they rented a flat in a large Victorian villa at 3a Longton Avenue Sydenham. Cyril and Vi, both retired clerical officers later moved into a semi-detached house in West Wickham, at 40 The Mead.

Woolley died at Guys Hospital in 1979 leaving the house to Vi, where she died of a coronary in May 1985 aged eighty-four –leaving probate of £53,794. Leslie was the informant on both death certificates.

After the war, still in his early twenties Leslie joined the civil service as a tax officer. He married twenty-year old Eileen Widdows in April 1948 at St Mary's Church, Ewell; a daughter arrived the same year. In 1952 perhaps under financial pressure, he became involved in serious litigation, which affected his marriage and career. [35] By the time he moved to Sydenham, his marriage had been dissolved.

In his mid-forties, now a taxation accountant he lived for a while in Wickham Chase, West Wickham where he met Sheila Cronin a schoolteacher some nine years younger. They married at Bromley registry office in May 1969, with his mother as witness. They lived in West Common Road Hayes Bromley; both appear on the 2002 local electoral register.

Little information has emerged about his youngest son Archie, but I understand he was an intense and intellectual man, known to his intimates as Glyn. [36] He became a teacher, married Marjorie and they had two children. He retired to Isfield a Sussex village near Lewes, and died of a coronary in a Crowborough nursing home October 2002.

The Welsh National Opera

Sixteen years after Tom's death the Chorus of the Welsh National Opera finally became professional in 1973, moving to its first permanent home -the new Wales Millennium Centre in Cardiff Bay in December 2004.

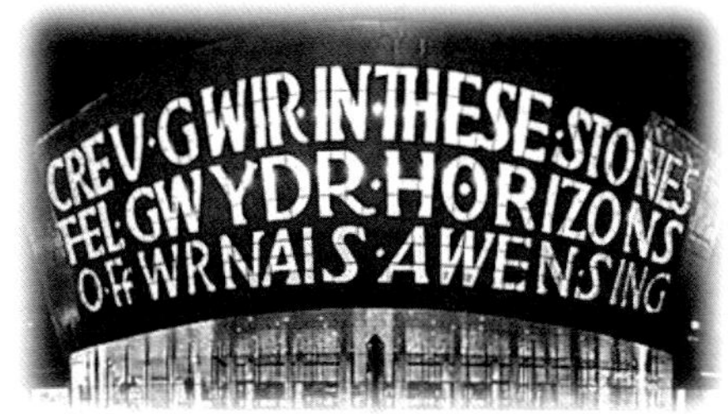

Mollie Hair now Hair Russell, had been coached by Idloes Owen, and one-time WNO principal dancer. She had choreographed the company's corps de ballet and also performed as principal soprano. Pre-war she had trained at *Sadler's Wells*, and the *Cone School of Dancing*. Lily Cone was a children's examiner of the Royal Academy of Dancing. [37]

Mollie once cast Tom in the comic opera *The Bartered Bride* at the New Theatre Cardiff in 1955. Fifty years later, at the age of ninety (June 2011) she still remembered Tom Morgan, describing him as: "*a big, rugged, handsome man, ... a lovely man and great fun to work with...*"

...and he was, my Welsh uncle.

Mollie Hair in the 'Bartered Bride'

Tom on his way to perform in 'The Bartered Bride' at the New Theatre Cardiff

Notes

1 To begin at the Beginning

[1] *A Cardiff Divorce Case, a Shocking Story* –ran the press headline. The proceedings appeared in an article syndicated to the *South Wales Echo*, *South Wales Daily News*, *Western Mail* and *Cardiff Times*, April 21, 1887. Elizabeth declared on oath Josiah had behaved *"like a brute"* throughout their marriage

[2] Sixty-odd years later, the spoil tip from this colliery, led to the catastrophic Aberfan disaster. One morning, at 9.15 am, on 21 October 1966 the tip slid silently down the mountain above the village killing 116 children and 28 adults as it engulfed the local junior school and other buildings. Tommy Morgan's youngest son Bernard *(1911-1973)* a miner, helped in the rescue

[3] Betty Sleeman *(1918-2011)* correspondence December 2006

2 Picking primroses

[4] Oral recollections Lena Dann *(1918-1994)* and notes Betty Sleeman

[5] Russ made a private recording for his mother in a Voice-O-Graph booth whilst serving in post-war Germany. He sang the Irish ballad *The Rose of Tralee;* his young voice sung 'a cappella', would always bring a tear to Mag's eye whenever it was played

3 The house on the corner

[6] David Morgan (no relation) was a family-run department store in Cardiff noted for its service. It ceased trading in 2005 after 125 years. The young Michael Aspel worked in the store in the 1950s before moving into television as a newsreader (*David Morgan, illustrated history 1879-2005*, pages 81, 128)

[7] Kardomah Cafés, a chain of coffee shops in England, Wales, and a few in Paris, popular from the early 1900s until the 1960s. They featured live entertainment provided by string quartets. The Swansea café opened in 1910 and continues in Portland Street. Cardiff opened in 1929, but now closed

[8] After Josiah married Sarah Shepherd, she became known as 'Aunty Sarah' to the original Morgan grandchildren –never grandma. She produced five children, they all lived in Cardiff. Hilda, Hubert (*Fairwater)* worked on the railways, Gladys, Mable (*Roath*) and Gwennie (*Roath*). Hilda owned a café in Bute Street; Gwennie had an interest in *The New Continental* once a fashionable restaurant in Queen Street. It was managed by Julian Hodge –a Welsh financier, during WW2 on behalf of the interned Italian family. After Sarah died (1921) Gladys looked after Josiah until his death (1935), she had married Percy Salway (1923) before moving to Malefant Street in Cathays

[9] Leichner grease sticks are the basis of all theatric.al make up. A need emerged for new more skilful application techniques when stage gas and electric lighting appeared. Ludwig Leichner *(1836-1912)*, a Wagnerian opera singer, began commercially producing a non-toxic greasepaint stick in 1873, easing the application of makeup

[10] Mollie Hair Russell. *https://barryrussell.wordpress.com/2011/06/16/99/*

[11] Augustus John *(1878-1961)*, biography, Michael Holroyd, page 70

[12] Music critic and editor Kenneth Loveland's review, *South Wales Daily Argus* July 1956, he resigned in 1970 to concentrate on Music Criticism and Travel Writing. He was one of the main programme annotators for *The City of Birmingham Symphony Orchestra*, and the *BBC National Orchestra of Wales* See also his correspondence with *WNOC, National Library of Wales Archives GF/L12*
[13] When Mrs Hartman read Lady Brassey's reference, my mother was employed on the spot. She had dined with the Brassey's many times. See *Maud Coleno's Daughter, the life of Dorothy Hartman 1898-1957,* pages 312-3

4 The boy soldier -First World War

[14] *Boy Soldier of the Great War*, Richard Van Emden, page XIV, apart from changing their age many enlisted under false names making research difficult
[15] Family oral recollections Lena Dann, Betty Sleeman, and entries in Annie Morgan's *(1874-1945)* birthday book refers to: *Winnie Morgan born March 15th 1918; Leslie Morgan born July 30 1922 Tom's boy; Archie Morgan, born July 3 1924 Tom's boy;* and again *Winnie's baby John Payne born 23 Sept 1939*
[16] Source: *Royal College of Nursing - Register of Nurses in 1934: p1478, Registered No. 71318, Morgan, Winifred Muriel, 27 The Grove, Aberfan, Merthyr Tydfil Wales, November 24, 1933 London, St Mary Abbot's Hosp. London, 1928-1932, By Examination.* Possibly oblivious to this fact, Adrian Payne (grandson) felt his grandmother was a little frustrated with her life, from time to time and had remained unfulfilled in some way
[17] The 1939 Register, was a nation-wide collection to produce war-time Identity Cards, facilitate the issuing of ration books, administer conscription, division of labour, and to monitor and control the movement of the population caused by military mobilisation and mass evacuation
[18] Jill Peck *(1949-)* Bernard Morgan's daughter memories of Vi:, "*mam and her didn't get on, I believe she was the reason mam and Brian left and returned to Aberfan*"

5 To war, again -Second World War

[19] The Company Quartermaster Sergeant (CQMS) is the second most senior NCO non-commissioned officer in the British Army in charge of supplies. In infantry companies, the CQMS is always addressed as *"Colour Sergeant"*
[20] *Happy Odyssey*, Lt-Gen. Sir Carton De Wiart, page 190
[21] See full story*, Always To-Morrow, George G Harrap & Co. Ltd., London 1951*
[22] *Happy Odyssey*, Lt-Gen. Sir Carton De Wiart, page 194
[23] MI9, Military Intelligence Section 9, tasked with war-time escape and evasion, through resistance organisations and manufacturing various escape aids for POW's *(see MI9 Escape & Evasion 1939-45, The Bodley Head, 1979)*
[24] *Playing with Strife, The Autobiography of a Soldier*, Sir Philip Neame page 303
[25] *Happy Odyssey*, Lt-Gen. Sir Carton De Wiart, page 222
[26] *Ibid*, page 233
[27] *Playing with Strife, The Autobiography of a Soldier*, Sir Philip Neame page 325
[28] *Steady, Old Man! Don't You Know There's a War On?* Derek Bond, page 139
[29] *Ibid,* page 152,
[30] *Ibid,* pages 151-2,
[31] *Ibid,* pages 168-9

6 A blackbird sang

[32] Oral recollections and notes Lena Dann, Betty Sleeman

[33] The BBC used Blockley church and vicarage in 2012 as their location for the first TV series of *Father Brown*, based on G. K. Chesterton's fictional detective - now in its sixth series

7 Postscripts

[34] MI9 report June 1944, National Archives, Cat. Ref. WO/208/3320, explicit details appear in *The Vatican Pimpernel*, pages 109-112, Monsignor Hugh O'Flaherty was portrayed by Gregory Peck in the 1983 film *The Scarlet and the Black*. The hospital on Via Santo Stefano Rotundo was also the war-time home of self-exiled George Santayana *(1863–1952)*, Spanish born American philosopher, poet and novelist

[35] On 11 Nov 1952, a newspaper article appeared headed: *Tax Man Accused of Taking Bribes*, with the verdict delivered nine-days later. Leslie Wallace Morgan, a 30 year old Inland Revenue tax officer based in Epsom, with a wife and four year old child, was sentenced to three years in prison for corruption

[36] Adrian Payne, family recollections Payne-Down family *Ancestry.com*

[37] The Cone founded in 1919, (studio above Lilly & Skinner's shoe shop Oxford Street), merged in 1939 forming the Cone-Ripman school, moving to Tring Park during the war, becoming the Arts Educational School. Today known as *Tring Park School for the Performing Arts*, notable alumni include: *John Gilpin, Sarah Brightman,* and *Dame Julie Andrews*

Tom lived variously at the following addresses

1898	*40 Cardiff Road Merthyr Vale*
1905	*8 Station Terrace Merthyr Vale*
1914-18	*WW1*
1918	*8 Station Terrace Merthyr Vale*
1922	*48 Moy Road Aberfan*
1924	*4 Hoel Treharne Abergwynfi*
1930c	*27 The Grove Aberfan*
1937c	*8 Clyde Street Adamsdown Cardiff*
1939-45	*WW2*
1945	*8 Clyde Street Adamsdown Cardiff*
1947	*25 Dogfield Street Cathays Cardiff*
1954	*105 Dogfield Street Cathays Cardiff*
1957	*2 Northwick Terrace Blockley*

Acknowledgements and Sources

The Morgan family archive of photographs & private papers, author's *Lett's* school-boy diaries *(1954-7*), additional un-published material in Annie Morgan, *(1874-1945)* birthday book; conversations and correspondence with Lena Dann, mother *(1918-1994),* Betty Sleeman, cousin *(1918-2011)* eldest daughter of Mag Rees (née Morgan). My thanks for further contributions from Jill Peck *(1949-)* Bernard Morgan's daughter; and Adrian Payne *(1965-)* Tom Morgan's great-grandson

Open sources: BMD, parish records, census and electoral rolls, military records, divorce, wills and probate, various published family-tree information

Wikipedia references: Mai Jones *(1899–1960)*; 255th Tunnelling Company; Welsh National Opera; Idloes Owen *(1894–1954)*; Merthyr Vale; Vincigliata (*Campo 12)* & Stalag VII-A ; Church of St Peter and St Paul, Blockley

Ancestry.com: Payne-Down family records, courtesy of Adrian Payne; Mollie Hair Russell's reminiscing on her early WNO operatic career, courtesy of *barryrussell.wordpress.com /2011/06/16/99/*; records of Welsh National Opera performances *1955-56,* courtesy of the *New Theatre* Cardiff Archive, *www.newtheatrecardiff.co.uk;* Tom's war records, *www.forces-war-records.co.uk, 1939* Register, *www.findmypast.co.uk* in association with The National Archives; Merthyr valley archives courtesy of *www.alangeorge.co.uk;* BNA-British Newspaper Archive *www.britishnewspaperarchive.co.uk;* record of civil divorce proceedings, *Morgan v Morgan & Thomas*, High Court of Justice, Probate Divorce and Admiralty division, petition 2 Dec 1885, final decree 8 Nov 1887 *National Archives*

Selected quotes: books, lyrics, poems and speeches gratefully acknowledged.

Under Milk Wood, (1954) Dylan Thomas *(1914-1953)* courtesy of David Higham Associates, administrators of the estate of Dylan Thomas; *The Primrose,* Robert Herrick *(1591-1674)* The Oxford Book of English Verse *1250–1900*, Arthur Quiller-Couch, Ed; Part of the transcript of Neville Chamberlain's declaration of war, 1939 courtesy BBC archives; *1919; Tommy (1892),* Rudyard Kipling *(1865–1936),* courtesy National Trust; *Keep the Home-Fires Burning (Till the Boys Come Home) (1914)* composed by Ivor Novello *(1893–1951)* with words by Lena Guilbert Ford; *Addlestrop (1917)* Edward Thomas *(1878-1917); "History with its flickering lamp*"… lines from a speech made to the House of Commons, 12 November 1940 by Winston Churchill *(1874–1965); We'll keep a welcome* lyrics collaboration Mai Jones, Lyn Joshua and James Harper *(1940)*; the score © 1949 courtesy of Lawrence Wright Music Co Ltd., EMI Music Publishing Ltd

Images

The author's family collections, others gratefully acknowledged.

Chapter 1 *To begin at the beginning:* Pencoed castle courtesy *www.castlewales.com*, photo copyright ©Laurie Oliver and site ©Jeffrey L. Thomas; Castell Coch, courtesy of *www.shireswalk.com*; Castello di Vincigliata, *(2011)* author, *(1946)* courtesy of the late Lt.-Gen. Sir Philip Neame's estate and book, *Playing with Strife;* the two Tom's, father and son as colliers, *(c.1911)* kind permission of Jill Peck; Station Terrace Merthyr Vale courtesy of *Alangeorge.co.uk*
Chapter 2 *Picking primroses:* woodland primroses, courtesy of Emorsgate Seeds, *www.wildseed.co.uk;* Badminton Old Vicarage *(2011)* courtesy, ©Ray Bird Creative Commons *www.geograph.org.uk/photo/5219321;* Cardiff images, courtesy of *Wales-on-line.co.uk archive*
Chapter 3 *The house on the corner*: Idloes Owen courtesy of *www.merthyr-history.com*; Churchman's cigarettes, courtesy *Wikipedia Commons*; and advertisement *www.historyworld.co.uk;* Leichner stage make up, courtesy of *www.backstageshop.co.uk;* Derek Bond, courtesy of *www.filmweb.pl,* publicity photo copyright unknown; New Theatre Cardiff *c.1950s* image source unknown; *Happy Odyssey* paperback cover, image courtesy of *Pan books*; Cardiff images courtesy of *Pinterest, Old Cardiff*
Chapter 4 *The boy soldier*: images of Vimy ridge: courtesy of *Wikipedia commons* and *Imperial War Museum*; Image of Ralph, Winnie and Vi *(1970)* kind permission of Adrian Payne
Chapter 5 *To war, again:* Erwin Rommel, with the 15th Panzer Division between Tobruk and Sidi Omar 1941, courtesy of *rarehistoricalphotos.com*; Maj.-General Sir Adrian Carton de Wiart 1941, courtesy of the late John F. Leeming's estate and book *Always To-morrow*, page 80; Lt-General Sir Richard O'Connor: courtesy of *ww2db.com*; Lt-General Philip Neame 1941, courtesy of the late Lt-General Neame's estate and book *Playing with Strife*; Maj.-General Michael Gambier-Parry, courtesy of Michael Todhunter; brief article on PG 12 Vincigliata, and group image courtesy of *The Prisoner of War*, journal of the prisoner of war Department of the British Red Cross and St John, St James's Palace, London, SW1, June 1943; Stalag XVIIA, courtesy of *www.allstalags.com* and Jim Lankford, deputy national historian *www.moosburg.org;* Lancaster bombers O*peration Exodus Wikipedia Commons*
Chapter 6 *A blackbird sang*: Cardiff General Station, courtesy Roger Cornfoot, *Wikipedia Commons*; Blockley, street exterior towards tower of St Peter & St Paul's, courtesy Alan Taylor *(1999), places.wishful-thinking.org.uk*; churchyard & interior courtesy of *churchcrawler.blogspot.co.uk;* High Street, courtesy of Frances Frith collection
Chapter 7 *Postscript:* Millennium Centre in Cardiff, (Opera House) courtesy of Thomas Deusing, *classical-iconoclast.blogspot.co.uk*; Mollie Hair (in *Carmen*) and theatre poster with kind permission of *barryrussell.wordpress.com;* images of Winnie & Ralph Payne, kind permission of Adrian Payne

Selected bibliography

BOND, Derek, M.C., *Steady, Old Man! Don't You Know There's a War On?* Leo Cooper (Pen & Sword) 1990

CARTON De WIART, Lt-Gen. Sir Adrian, V.C., K.B.E., C.M.G., D.S.O., *Happy Odyssey,* Jonathan Cape Ltd, 1950, (PAN paperback 1956), re-printed by Pen & Sword Books, 2007

COOMBES, B. L., *Twenty Tons of Coal*, The Penguin Book of Welsh Short Stories, Ed. Alun Richards, 1976

DANN, John, *Maud Coleno's Daughter, the life of Dorothy Hartman 1898-1957,* Matador 2017

FAWKES, Richard, *Welsh National Opera,* Julia MacRae Books 1986

FLEMING, Brian, *The Vatican Pimpernel*, Skyhorse Publishing Inc. 2012

FOOT, M.R.D. & LANGLEY, J.M., *MI9 Escape & Evasion 1939-45,* The Bodley Head 1979

GRANT GRIEVE, Capt. W., *Tunnellers: The story of the Tunnelling Companies, Royal Engineers, during the World War,* with Bernard Newman (Contributor), first published 1936, new paperback edition Naval and Military Press 2004

HARGEST, Brig. James, C.B.E., D.S.O. M.C., *Farewell Campo .12,* Michael Joseph Ltd. 1945 (Published posthumously)

HOLROYD, Michael, *Augustus John,* biography, William Heinemann Ltd., London, 1976, revised edition Pimlico 2001

LEE, Brian, *David Morgan, The Family Store, An Illustrated History 1879-2005*, Breedon Books 2005

LYNNE, Gillian, *A Dancer in Wartime: One girl's journey from the Blitz to Sadler's Wells*, Chatto & Windus, London 2011

LEEMING, John F., *Always To-Morrow,* George G Harrap & Co., London 1951

NEAME, Lt-Gen. Sir Philip, V.C., K.B.E., C.B., D.S.O., *Playing with Strife, The Autobiography of a Soldier,* George G Harrap & Co. Ltd. 1947

RANFURLY The Countess of, *To War with Whitaker, The wartime diaries of The Countess of Ranfurly 1939 -1945,* William Heinemann Ltd., London 1994

VAN EMDEN, Richard, *Boy Soldiers of the Great War*, Bloomsbury 2012

The Morgan family

The *cyfarwydd* believed the paternal line of Tom's ancestry is traced from the tenth-century Welsh king *Morgan Hen ab Owain (Morgan the Old).* He briefly united the former kingdoms of Gwent and Glywysing in 942 under the name of Morgannwg, todays' Glamorgan. Continuing through many (impoverished) cadet branches of Tredegar and Pencoed Morgan's to the present.

|

David Morgan = Eliza Gronow
b. c1827 Whitchurch, Fireman, Blacksmith d.1860s?
b. c1821 Llandaff m.1849 widower in Roath c1881, d.c1894, Dressmaker, two children: Josiah, John (1852-96)

Thomas Thomas = Ann Jones
b.1809 *Aberdare m. 1833-4? Moulder/Brick manufacturer, d.?*
b.1814 Pentrych d.? eight children: Thomas (1834), Eleanor (1835), Mary (1838), Morgan (1841), Catherine (1844), Jane (1843), William (1850), Elizabeth

|

Josiah *(Jesaiah, Jesse, Jos)* Morgan = *1st m* Elizabeth Thomas = *2nd m* Sarah Shepherd
(eldest) b. Radyr, 1849 d.1936, Puddler -Iron Works c.1871 Weigher -Ironworks c.1881, Railway Guard c.1891, Bute Dock Pilot c.1895, Railway train driver c 1901
bi-lingual -youngest daughter, b. Newbridge, 12 Feb 1854, m. Jun 1870, divorced 1887, m. Harry Stacey, 1891 d. 23 July 1897, Dressmaker
b. St Brides Super Ely 1869 m.1889 d. 1921, Five children: Hilda (1891), Hubert (1893), Gladys (1895), Mable (1897), Gwennie (1899)

Three children (first marriage)

|

David Reginald Morgan
bi-lingual b. Radyr 8 Oct 1870 d.1925 Coal tipper, m. Phoebe Davies 1892, served 3rd Welch Regiment WW1

Urina *(Lina)* Blanch Morgan
bi-lingual b. Radyr 9 Nov 1871 d.1931 m. [1] John Jarrett 1890 d.1895,[2] William Henderson 1897,[3]Jim Wheeler 1911,[4] Bertie Newman 1929

Thomas John Morgan
bi-lingual b. Radyr 28 Mar 1873 d.1939

|

Thomas *(Tommy)* John Morgan = Annie Wakely
b. *Radyr 1873 d.1939 Coal miner (Hewer) (Tommy Cardiff)*
b. Mountain Ash 1874 m.1895 d.1945 7th child of Henry & Margaret, unofficial village herbalist and midwife, siblings: William (1850), George (1858), John (1864), Alfred (1868), Henry (1870), Harriett (1871), Arthur (1875), Fred (1878)

Nine children

|

Margaret *(Mag)* Elizabeth Morgan
(Eldest), b. Merthyr Vale 1895 m. Will Rees 1916, d.1963 Domestic servant, Dressmaker, four children: Betty (1919-2011), Donald (1921-1991), Russell (1926-1980), Margaret (1930-2017)

Thomas *(Tom)* Henry Morgan
b. Merthyr Vale 1898 d.1957 Coal miner (Hewer), Composer, Painter, Labourer, Soldier, Storekeeper & dispatch clerk Opera chorister

Seven younger siblings: [No. children]
Arthur (1899-1973) m. Laura Booth 1919 [3]
Archie (1902-1966) m. Kitty Arnott 1930 [1]
George (1905-1968) m. Muriel Jones 1929 [2]
Maudie (1907-1974) m. Jack Pritchard 1928 [2]
Jess (1909-1960) m. Enid Owers 1939 [2]
Bernard (1911-1973) m. Morfydd Jones 1940 [2]
Lena Gwen (1918-1994) m. Jack Dann 1942 [1]

|

Thomas *(Tom)* Henry Morgan = Ethel Violet *(Vi)* Tinsley
b.12 Feb 1898 m.7 Feb 1922 d.14 Mar 1957 (59yrs)
b. Sudbury, Suffolk May 1900 d.1985 (84yrs), Nurse, Clerk, parents: Thomas (1876-1925) & Florence (1878-1950s), sisters: Doris (1904-), Grace (1910-)

Three children

Winnie was not Tom's child, but unofficially adopted, taking the name Morgan when he married her mother four years later. 'Vi' had talked of divorcing Tom since at least 1945, and they lived apart from around that time.

|

Winifred *(Winnie)* Muriel Tinsley
b. Blaenrhondda 1918 d.1983 (65yrs)
|
Winnie (Win) m. Ralph Payne 1937 two children: John b.1939 Keith b.1944

Leslie Wallace Morgan
b. Aberfan 1922 d. after 2002? (80+yrs?)
|
Leslie 1st m. Eileen Widdows 1948 one daughter Lynne, m. dissolved, 2nd m. Sheila Cronin 1969 no children?

Archie *(Glyn)* Morgan
b. Abergwynfi 1924 d.2002 (78yrs)
|
Archie m. Marjorie name? date? two children Julian, one other?

Welsh National Opera

From the first production of *Cavallieria Rusticana* at the *Prince of Wales Theatre* Cardiff in April 1946, the company steadily built its repertoire and reputation.

By the spring of 1952 it had extended its performances to the *Empire Theatre* Swansea, and in the autumn performed *Nabucco* in Cardiff –to critical acclaim. Their first visit outside the Principality was to Bournemouth in 1953, and a year late established a new home at the *New Theatre* in Cardiff. In 1955 it premiered in London at *Sadler's Well Theatre* in the summer, and continued the following autumn in Cardiff these would be Tom's last seasons.

7 October 1952

The production of *Nabucco* at the Sophia Gardens Cardiff –the first major performance in Britain that century, was critically acclaimed, immediately classing the WNO amongst the leading opera companies in Britain.

PRINCE OF WALES THEATRE
CARDIFF
Box Office open 10 a.m. to 9 p.m. Telephone : 3528

Commencing MONDAY 8th MAY—FOR TWO WEEKS
Nightly at 7 p.m. Matinees : Saturdays at 2.30 p.m.

The
WELSH NATIONAL OPERA COMPANY
(with the support of the Arts Council of Great Britain)
in the following repertoire :

TALES OF HOFFMANN	Monday, 8th ; Wednesday, 10th ; Friday, 12th ; and Matinee on Saturday, 13th May.
FAUST	Tuesday, 9th and Thursday, 11th May.
THE BARTERED BRIDE	Saturday, 13th ; Tuesday, 16th ; Friday, 19th ; and Matinee on Saturday, 20th May.
DIE FLEDERMAUS	Monday, 15th ; Wednesday, 17th ; Thursday, 18th ; and Saturday, 20th May.

*

Guest Artistes :
Gerald Davies, Edmund Donlevy, Howell Glynne, Gabriel Todd

Principals :
Nancy Bateman, Elizabeth Bowen, Zoe Cresswell Margaret Glyn, Joan Stephens, Margaret Williams, Mollie Hair, Phyllis Ash-Child, Patti Lewis, Evan Ellis, Frank James, Arnold Davies, Bruce Wilson, Geoffrey Davies

SYMPHONY ORCHESTRA
Leader : Alfred Barker.

Conductors : Charles Mackerras ; Leo Quayle (by permission of the Administrators of Sadlers Wells) and Arwel Hughes.

Operas produced by Norman Jones and N. John Donaldson (by permission of the Administrators of Sadlers Wells).

> – *"it would be impossible to find a single weakness in last night's cast"*, commented the critic of the Western Mail.
>
> *"The stellar honours for the evening went not to one of the soloists but to the eighty-strong chorus. Verdi's swinging music was sung with a passion and fervour that had not been heard on the British operatic stage before. Their lack of vocal inhibition as they launched into each chorus with an emotion, a 'hwyl', usually reserved for rugby international at Cardiff Arms Park, reaching a magnificent climax…turned what might have been just and interesting resurrection of a long-lost opera into a triumph."*
>
> *Welsh National Opera*, 1986, pages 34-5

London – summer 1955

First season a week in July performing at *Sadler's Wells Theatre* Islington.

Cardiff - autumn 1955

26 September

Cavalleria Rusticana/ I Pagliacci /

Starring: Lilian Prosser-Evans, Tano Ferendinos, Patti Lewis, Elwyn Adams, Muriel Poynton, Arnold Davies, Una Hale, Victor White, William Edwards, Tegwyn Short, WNO Company, Bournemouth Symphony Orchestra

27 September
Nabucco /
Starring: Ruth Packer, Pauline Faull, Hervey Alan, Roderick Jones, Tano Ferendinos, Charles Groves, Tegwyn Short, Leslie Wicks, WNO Company, Bournemouth Symphony Orchestra

28 September
Die Fledermaus /
Starring: Jean Stevens, Zoe Cresswell, Howell Glynne, Edmund Donlevy, Frank James, Arnold Davies, WNO Company, Bournemouth Symphony Orchestra

29 September
Faust /
WNO Company, Bournemouth Symphony Orchestra

30 September
Tosca /
Starring: Kyra Vane, Walter Midgley, Roderick Jones, WNO Company, Bournemouth Symphony Orchestra

1 October
Bartered Bride /
WNO Company, Bournemouth Symphony Orchestra

2 October
La Boheme /
Starring: Patricia Bartlett, Walter Midgley, WNO Company, Bournemouth Symphony Orchestra

3 October
La Boheme /
Starring: Patricia Bartlett, Walter Midgley, WNO Company, Bournemouth Symphony Orchestra

4 October
Sicilian Vespers /
Starring: Ruth Packer, Brychan Powell, WNO Company, Bournemouth Symphony Orchestra

5 October
Tosca /
Starring: Kyra Vane, Walter Midgley, Roderick Jones, WNO Company, Bournemouth Symphony Orchestra

6 October
Rigoletto /
WNO Company, Bournemouth Symphony Orchestra

7 October
Faust /
WNO Company, Bournemouth Symphony Orchestra

8 October
Cavalleria Rusticana/ I Pagliacci /
Starring: Lilian Prosser-Evans, Tano Ferendinos, Patti Lewis, Elwyn Adams, Muriel Poynton, Arnold Davies, Una Hale, Victor White, William Edwards, Tegwyn Short, WNO Company, Bournemouth Symphony Orchestra

8 October
Nabucco /
Starring: Ruth Packer, Pauline Faull, Hervey Alan, Roderick Jones, Tano Ferendinos, Charles Groves, Tegwyn Short, Leslie Wicks, WNO Company, Bournemouth Symphony Orchestra

London – summer 1956

The second London season, a week in July performing Verdi opera's *Nabucco* and *I Lombardi* together with Wagner's *Lohengrin,* at *Sadler's Wells Theatre* Islington.

Cardiff - autumn 1956

1 October
I Lombardi /
Starring: Bryan Drake, Paul Asciak, Rosina Raisbeck, Lillian Prosser-Evans, Leonard John, Tegwyn Short, Lwyn Adams, Alfred Hallett, Patti Lewis, Bournemouth Symphony Orchestra, Warwick Braithwaite,

2 October
La Boheme /
Starring: Walter Midgley, Ronald Lewis, Bryan Drake, Michael Langdon, Tegwyn Short, Vivian Davies, Emlyn Smith, Ben Williams, Zoe Cresswell, Patricia Bartlett

5 October
Tosca /
Starring: Victoria Elliott, Walter Midgley, Roderick Jones, Bryan Drake, William H Thomas, Mervyn Meyrick, Tom A Morgan, Vivian Davies

8 October
The Barber of Seville /
Starring: Tano Ferendinos, Howell Glyne, Barbara Wilson, William Dickie, Michael Langdon, Vivian Davies, Patti Lewis, Tom A Morgan

Welsh words explained

With grateful acknowledgement of the GPC - Geiriadur Prifysgol Cymru
The standard dictionary of the Welsh language, published online by the University of Wales

Cwtch, a Welsh word with no literal English translation. There are plenty of similar words, such as 'cuddle', 'snuggle' and 'hug', but none share quite the same affectionate sentiment as a *cwtch.*
Ask a Welsh person what a *cwtch* (rhymes with 'butch') is and often they'll give you a fond smile – because it is evocative – it has the magical quality of transporting someone back to the safety of their childhood. This corresponds with the word's other meaning, which is a place to safely store things – if you give someone a *cwtch*; you're figuratively giving them a 'safe place'.

Hiraeth is a another for which there is no direct English translation, but translates to a homesickness tinged with grief or sadness over the lost or departed. Best illustrated by the lyrics to Tom's score: *"…This land of song will keep a welcome/And with a love that never fails /We'll kiss away each hour of Hiraeth…"* pronounced *Hee-ryeth.*

Hwyl, describes emotional fervour, a complex and intangible quality of passion together with a sense of belonging that isn't easy to translate, but which has been said to sum up *Welshness* in a word.

The Geiriadur Prifysgol Cymru: states *"a healthy physical or mental condition, good form, one's right senses, wits; tune (of a musical instrument); temper, mood, frame of mind; nature, disposition; degree of success achieved in the execution of a particular task etc.; ("put a bit hwyl into it boy"), fervour (especially religious), ecstasy, unction, gusto, zest; characteristic musical intonation or sing-song cadence formerly much in vogue in the perorations of the Welsh pulpit."*
Pronounced *hoil*, most broadly, *hwyl* refers to a person's mood.

Author

Born in Gwaunfarren House Merthyr Tydfil, during the Second World War. The same summer the Castle cinema with its Christie theatre organ, was screening the *Bogart & Bergman* film *Casablanca* to packed houses. Both buildings now demolished in a vanishing Wales.

A Welsh childhood followed in the mining village of Merthyr Vale, then variously in the Cardiff suburbs of Adamsdown, Rhiwbina and Cathays, before moving to Surrey at the age of thirteen.

He has interests in family and military history, rugby and all things maritime. He lives in Cornwall - beachcombing with his Labrador.

Other books

Struck by Lightning (2012)
A sailor's first-hand story about a Second World War fighting ship
HMS Lightning 1941–1943 (with Eric Gilroy)

Thomas Cook's Rugby Club (2013)
Its life and times 1910-1966
(Paperback revised edition)

Maud Coleno's Daughter (2017)
The life of Mayfair hostess Dorothy Hartman 1898-1957
(Hardback)

Rugger Shorts (2017)
Reflections on the amateur game -An anthology of rugby trivia
(Paperback)

Mr Bridgman's Accomplice (2018)
Long Ben's Coxswain 1660-1722
(Paperback)

'Pwy sy'n dioddef wedi goresgyn'
(Who endured has overcome)

Old Welsh proverb

ND - #0109 - 080726 - C0 - 234/156/4 - PB - 9781784565978 - Gloss Lamination